QUICK WINS!

Accelerating
School Transformation
through Science,
Engagement,
and Leadership

QUICK WINS!

Accelerating School Transformation through Science, Engagement, and Leadership

Paul "Paulie" Gavoni, Ed.D.

Manuel "Manny" Rodriguez, M.S.

Copyright © 2016 by ABA Technologies, Inc.

All rights reserved. This book or any portion thereof may not be reproduced or used in any manner whatsoever without the express written permission of the publisher except for the use of brief quotations in a book review or scholarly journal.

First Printing: 2016

ISBN 978-1-365-53640-3

ABA Technologies, Inc.
150 West University Blvd.
Melbourne, FL 32901
info@abatechnologies.com
321-674-8326

www.abatechnologies.com

Ordering Information:

Special discounts are available on quantity purchases by corporations, associations, educators, and others. For details, contact the publisher at the above listed address.

Table of Contents

Acknowledgements
Chapter 1: Fresh Paint and Targeted Misbehavior 1
Chapter 2: Quick Wins Require Leadership (Round 1)..7
Chapter 3: Quick Wins Require *QuickWOCs* 15
Chapter 4: Quick Wins Need S.M.A.R.T. Goals and Data 29
Chapter 5: Quick Wins Require Communication 45
Chapter 6: Quick Wins Require Positive Leadership (Round 2) 61
Chapter 7: Quick Wins: Important Strategies and Tactics 79
Chapter 8: Quick Wins in Action: Improving School Climate and Culture 85
Final Thoughts 121
References 123

Acknowledgements

Throughout the journey of writing *Quick Wins*, many individuals supported us both professionally and personally. Our families and friends gave us flexibility to write, provided the opportunity to bend their ears with our describing Quick Wins and the intricacies within the stories, and they were sounding boards providing both positive and constructive feedback. To our families and friends, thank you.

We would like to extend our sincerest thanks to John Lynch for his 3+3+60 contribution to our Quick Wins book. A former assistant superintendent, John is a remarkably accomplished turnaround principal as he has transformed schools at the elementary, middle, and high school level.

To former turnaround principal and nationally recognized consultant, Dr. Scott Neil. Scott and Paul collaborated to develop and successfully apply the very first system of Quick Wins that eventually led to the development of this book. As the President of School Leadership Solutions, Scott has gone on to lead multiple teams across the country in their school turnaround processes.

A sincere thanks to turnaround principal Jennifer Hedeen for her very valuable contribution to the *Customer Service and Curb Side Appeal* piece.

Finally, to ABA Technologies, Manny's employer but even more so, a group of colleagues and friends who were ready to support us in every way possible, and they came through in spades. The team exemplifies professionalism and thought leadership in bringing behavioral science to the world. To our friends at ABA

Tech, thank you. A special thanks to Emily Meyer for her thoughtful review of the early draft of the book as a former teacher and behavior analysts, April Rowland for her creative thinking in the cover art of the book, and Shannon Biagi for her attention to detail in making this become a reality for publication. We also want to extend a special thanks to the practitioners, researchers, and educations in the field of Applied Behavior Analysis and Organizational Behavior Management. These professionals are paving the way for positive change across the globe, serving various needs such development disabilities, organizational change, community wide improvements, and education to name a few. The work and effort of so many has influenced us to practice with integrity and focus. We tip our hats to these professionals, and simply appreciate their work to make a difference in this world.

Thanks

Paulie and Manny

Chapter 1: Fresh Paint and Targeted Misbehavior

A principal once took over an impoverished elementary school characterized by low achievement and high frequency of misbehavior. Parents were disillusioned with the school. The staff, burdened with pressure to improve, had low morale and high motivation to pursue greener pastures. However, many staff decided to stay, to see what this new principal could offer. Recognizing that he was under a microscope, the principal knew he must do something fast to strengthen belief in his vision and motivate his staff in any change initiative. Not only did he want staff members to believe in his vision—he needed his staff to believe in themselves.

Prior to their first day back, he had the school freshly painted. He felt it was important for staff to immediately see that a positive change had occurred. When teachers and staff returned from summer break, he asked what changes *they* would like to see. A major theme that emerged was *incidents of misbehavior.*

"We can't teach like we want to, with all the issues across campus that are overflowing into our classrooms," they told him. The principal, after hearing their passionate concerns, decided to concentrate initial effort in two areas: (1) students' arrival at school, and (2) lunchtime in the cafeteria. These specific focus areas, he discovered, were where the misbehavior occurred most, and where his staff struggled most to handle it. Though many teachers complained of misbehavior in the classroom, he believed that lunch and arrival times could be immediately transformed in such a way that it would also positively impact behavior in the classroom. His reasoning was that behavior in the classroom should improve as students would be more likely to enter calm and learning ready

To initiate this change, the principal provided brief training to the staff who supervised the cafeteria and arrivals—training on specific corrective procedures to follow when misbehavior occurred. Following the training, the principal asked his leadership team to keep their schedules open during arrival time and lunchtime. The leadership's role was threefold—(1) walk around—be present, (2) engage with the staff managing these situations, and (3) thank staff for being at their post, praising any positive interactions observed during these times.

If misbehavior occurred, the principal asked the leadership not to intervene with students directly, but rather coach the staff on the specific corrective procedures taught to them during the training. Once the coaching was completed, the leader would request the staff to apply these strategies while the leader observed. If the strategies were applied effectively, the leader was to specifically praise what was done correctly, and then point out the impact of these strategies on student behavior.

Quick Wins

As the school year started, the principal began observing these areas. In the past, if students were running in the hallways during arrival time, they were told to "walk" by the attending staff. As part of the principal's plan, staff were no longer to say "walk." Instead, they were to say, "Walk back to where you began running." This strategy, called positive practice, slightly delayed the student who was attempting to transition somewhere fast. In addition, other students vicariously learned that running would result in having to walk back. Inside of one week, change was not only visible to staff, but parents and district personnel who supported the school were shocked at the obvious change.

The principal, after the first week of implementing the new strategies, decided to compare his new discipline data to previous years. To his pleasant surprise, there had been an 80% reduction in discipline referrals, a fact he immediately shared and celebrated with the staff and leadership team. After two weeks, the principal met with his leadership team to assess and target a few more changes that would have a positive—and visible—impact on staff and student behaviors.

At the end of his first year, this principal had moved his school two letter grades, staff morale and retention was the highest in the district, and parents and district administrators praised the school for their amazing turnaround.

How could some paint and a few simple protocols in common areas have such an impact on student achievement, retention, and morale? Two words: *Quick Wins! Quick Wins* are a science-based and replicable rocket fuel for school leaders to propel change and transformation initiatives beyond the "gravity" that prevented previous initiatives from even launching.

* * *

Change is often hard for those involved. Many people resist change, whether it is small or large. Unfortunately, this resistance often stalls change, leaving school leaders scratching their heads as they reflect on a year's worth of struggle with little to show for it.

Had many of these leaders possessed *Quick Win* strategies for building momentum, like the principal in our story did, they likely would have accelerated change initiatives and met or even exceeded achievement goals.

A Quick Win is an improvement that is visible, has immediate benefit, and can be delivered quickly. People want to see meaningful improvement. In most cases, these improvements are easily identifiable, as they are changes that could have, and should have, been made long ago.

A *Quick Win* does not have to be profound or have a long-term impact on your organization. However the best *Quick Wins* are long-lasting and leave a profound effect on people's interest and ability to make change happen that *will* have a long-term impact. One thing is certain: a *Quick Win* necessitates that people agree on the need for change, act together to make the change, and learn from the change. To make such change happen, *Quick Wins* require leadership.

Quick Wins is a leader-led approach. School transformation, or any large-scale changes, rely on specific actions of a leader. School leaders need to empower others to establish a school culture where people embrace and implement change. The need for school turnaround and the current struggles that are overwhelmingly common within the process require school leaders take an active role. Considering the common failures in school turnarounds and their root causes, leadership's role in launching any change becomes absolutely critical.

Our driving philosophies and practices in Quick Wins are grounded in deep experience at applying the science of human behavior in the workplace. This is formally known as Organizational Behavior Management (OBM). OBM applies a blend of applications, such as Social Learning Theory, Applied Behavior Analysis, and business management techniques to create the very core of *Quick Wins*. These foundations support our contention of the role leadership plays in creating a positive climate and culture for building and sustaining school transformation.

Quick Wins is no gimmick, nor a flavor of the month. Nor is it a silver bullet. *Quick Wins* gives you the critical building blocks for rapidly accelerating change by providing a platform for leaders to build upon. *Quick Wins* is based on science, applying evidence-based approaches to making change happen and last.

The goal of this book is to be a school leader's "grab and go" resource on how to build momentum for change. Whether you are a school district official, principal, assistant principal, dean, guidance counselor, or hold any number of administrative positions where you engage people to implement change, this book is intended for you. Reading *Quick Wins* will give you a clear understanding and actionable steps related to:

- Engaging the team to rally around *Quick Wins*
- The power of direct observations and conversations during turnarounds
- The importance of feedback to build trust, self-efficacy, and performance
- The use and role of goals in turnarounds
- Leadership's role in delivering effective communication and feedback
- Common *Quick Wins* that can improve misbehavior, staff performance, and the school's climate and culture

Chapter 2: Quick Wins Require Leadership (Round 1)

Schools have their own personality. (Some might expand that to "personality disorder"!) This is why every school requires a customized approach to achieving its desired transformation. And it is why a "one-size fixes all" approach can never work to achieve transformation at all schools.

However, there is one constant in all turnarounds. It is the constant that differentiates successful turnarounds from failures. It is what gets highlighted in the media, and talked about by parents and teachers alike. It is what truly sets the tone of the school turnaround process from the start. This constant is *leadership!*

School turnarounds require sound leadership action to rapidly motivate people to accelerate change. What a school leader does to make such change happen depends on the school's specific needs: Are students failing? Are teachers quitting? Is the building in disrepair? Is the school under-enrolled, leaving the district wondering if it should be shut down? Are leaders feeling unsupported by their district leaders?

Unfortunately, in most turnaround cases, there is not just one problem. This harsh reality drives many school leaders to try changing everything at once. Sadly, they get nowhere fast. We agree with Simon Sinek, leadership consultant and best-selling author of books such as *Start with Why: How Great Leaders Inspire Everyone to Take Action,* when he suggested, "It is better to go slow in the right direction than to go fast in the wrong direction."

In the first year of a turnaround, without any observable positive changes, teachers leave and stakeholders quickly begin to question the leadership because there is not enough support for any initiatives to develop a successful trend. Under these conditions, a few outcomes are almost certain—the leader is asked to leave, the school fails, and most importantly, the students fall far short of their potential.

In contrast to trying to do it all, *Quick Wins* is about taking a focused, carefully targeted stance for supporting a few key areas to make change—*visible* change—not only happen but stick. These successes earn the leader trust, buy-in, and a track record to engage in further change. The leader benefits further in implementing *Quick Wins* by developing self-efficacy, as staff gain confidence in their ability to reach goals through regular measurement and effective feedback.

The *Quick Wins* approach lays a strong foundation for the future, enabling leaders to achieve success along the way to school transformation.

People First . . . Programs Second

Richard Branson, the famed entrepreneur and owner of Virgin Airlines, once said, *"Clients do not come first. Employees come first. If you take care of the employees, they will take care of the clients."* It is surprising how many district and school leaders don't understand that people—employees—come before programs!

If the goal of education is to bring out the best in their students, then leaders must bring out the best in the teachers and staff who impact student achievement. The school community needs to be involved in the school turnaround process from day one. People don't want things "done to them." This leads to people working in compliance mode, and doing the bare minimum to keep others happy and avoid getting into trouble.

The most successful school leaders we have worked with understand that all stakeholders within a school community need to have their voice heard on how to proceed with any significant change initiative. Building teamwork and shared responsibility toward solving the various challenges of turning around a school fosters collaboration and strengthens relationships amongst the staff in ways that produce results for many more years than any single program. An invested staff will propel leadership much farther toward sustainable change than throwing dollars toward the latest technology program or curriculum that is supposed to fix everything.

It's all about trust. Programs will go nowhere if they lack buy-in and a sense of purpose. An effective school leader develops relationships built on mutual trust between themselves and the rest of the school community. Trust is not some mystical phenomenon requiring yearly trust-building exercises. Simply put, leaders who follow through on what they say are trusted. Trust is essential for solidifying the development of strong relationships; in addition to trusting in the leader, people who do not feel trusted *by* the leader will be less than willing to provide the extra effort it takes to make the school a place of high achievement for all. Schools where the staff lacks trust will have employees who focus on doing just enough to get by. In fact, some will even sabotage efforts and negatively impact a school's sense of connectedness and drive to become great.

Recognizing Quick Wins: The *Quick Win Matrix*

Leaders will be able to recognize a *Quick Win* based on the *Quick Win* matrix evaluating any opportunities based on —

Impact, Visibility, Effort

Leaders of school turnarounds can stand confident in their decisions on which *Quick Wins* to tackle, using these criteria:

1. The ***Impact*** the *Quick Win* will bring to the school (scored 1 to 3)
2. The ***Visibility*** the *Quick Win* has to all who are watching the school's turnaround (scored 1 to 3)
3. The ***Effort*** to implement the *Quick Win* is achievable using available resources (scored 1 to 3)

The combination of Impact, Visibility, and Effort is what we have come to affectionately call a *Quick Win*!

Using the *Quick Win Matrix* (Figure 1) gives you a visual tool for prioritizing *Quick Wins*. The graphic illustrates the linkage among Impact, Visibility, and Effort:

- The higher the value of each, the better the *Quick Win*.
- It's not good enough just to hold high impact value —the *Quick Win* must be visible.
- If the *Quick Win* is high-impact and high-visibility, but the effort is too high, requiring lots of resources and possibly external support, the Quick Win may not be practical to pursue.

By focusing on **Impact, Visibility, and Effort**, the school leader is positioned to achieve *Quick Wins* for the turnaround.

Leaders working together with school staff can evaluate the impact, visibility, effort using a simple high-medium-low scale. As you can see, the ideal *Quick Win* has high impact, high visibility, and low-effort.

The ideal *Quick Win* is in the upper right box, because this meets all the criteria. Each *Quick Win* identified, as described throughout the remainder of the book, is categorized using the grid, multiplying each category to come to a final evaluation of the *Quick Wins* total score—the valid *Quick Win*.

Quick Wins

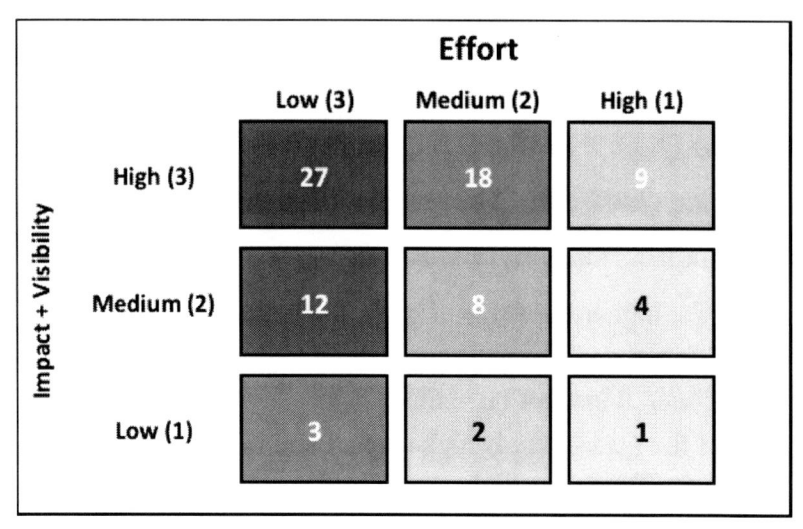

	Effort		
Impact + Visibility	Low (3)	Medium (2)	High (1)
High (3)	27	18	9
Medium (2)	12	8	4
Low (1)	3	2	1

Figure 1. The Quick Wins Matrix is scored using a 1, 2, or 3. Then the scores are multiplied together to determine the total value (up to 3x3x3, or 27). The ideal Quick Win—a 27— is in the upper-left box.

An example. One school administration team found themselves faced with two potential *Quick Wins*—improving the traffic pattern in the parking lot, and increasing communications between administrators regarding disruptive behavior. Administrators used the *Quick Wins Matrix*. Both potential *Quick Wins* were considered high-value. Specifically, the "parking lot" improved the impact of safety and efficiency, and "increasing communications" improved the value of communicating to mitigate problem behavior.

> ***Impact:*** Both *Quick Wins* received the highest score for value, 3 points.
> ***Visibility:*** Improving the parking lot traffic pattern would be seen by all who came to the school—specifically, during drop-off and pickup times—so this *Quick Win* got

a 3 for visibility. The second *Quick Win* of improving communications, however, was visible only to those who would be part of the communication (the principal, vice principal, security, and the teacher reporting the behavior problem). So this *Quick Win* got a 2 in visibility.

Effort: The venture to achieve each *Quick Win* was different. The resources to improve the communication (new technology, training, and a clear procedure) would take up to a month to complete, while the school parking lot traffic pattern could be done in a day. Thus, the school traffic pattern received an effort score of 3 (low effort), versus a score of 2 for communication.

In sum, the first *Quick Win* (parking lot traffic pattern) was prioritized with an overall score of 27 (3x3x3)—much higher than improving communication, which received a score of only 18 (3x2x3). Both *Quick Wins* were eventually accomplished. However, by prioritizing with the *Quick Wins Matrix*, school leaders were able to demonstrate real, immediate value to all stakeholders in a very short period of time.

Quick Wins

Chapter 3: Quick Wins Require *QuickWOCs*

Identifying *Quick Wins* can (and should!) be a *quick* process. The first step to identifying quick wins requires walking around, making direct observations and having conversations with people throughout the school. (This seems obvious, but sometimes folks miss the obvious, so it is essential to state.) The best turnarounds stand apart by this simple truth—*if I don't see it, hear it, or understand what's going on from those who live it, how can I effectively change it?*

Those in the know about daily happenings are the most critical in this step. To facilitate your *Observations* and *Conversations*, we have developed a tool called **QuickWOC.** (It's pronounced "quick walk," and **W** = Walking around, **O** = Observations, **C** = Conversations.

QuickWOC allows the leader to focus on specific areas and behaviors to walk around, observe, and converse when determining where a *Quick Win* could make a positive difference for students and teachers (The Doing What Works Library, 2015). Further, **QuickWOC** identifies other sources of information to help identify opportunities for improvement that may be addressed beyond the short term.

How to Use *QuickWOC*

QuickWOC has three parts:

    Part 1—Walkabout Observations
    Part 2—Other Sources
    Part 3—Performance Diagnostic Checklist

Part 1—Walkabout Observations. The walkabout is a walking tour of school facilities. This can be done in a group that includes administrators, teachers, and even students. If necessary, it can be done individually. Walk through the facility at different times during the school day, on different days, before and after school. Observe the elements listed in *QuickWOC* that might be corrected with immediate, focused, simple reforms. Note where you see problems occurring.

To focus your observations, *QuickWOC* suggests areas to observe and provides questions to guide your thinking. You may find additional areas to observe (e.g., portables, trailers, gymnasiums, auditoriums, etc.). The questions are based on common focus areas, such as arrival/dismissal, cafeteria, and classroom. These highly visible areas often are problematic in turnaround schools and can bring a *Quick Win*.

Part 2—Other Sources. Helps you seek input from other sources of information for identifying potential Quick Wins, such as reports from professionals who deliver services in the schools. The principal and leadership team may wish to collect information through meetings, informal conversations, and focus-group discussions with other school staff, parents, and possibly students. The principal and leadership team also can analyze data (discipline data, climate data, etc.) to identify areas of potential *Quick Wins*. The **QuickWOC** is also a great tool to use prior to the start of a new school year. During this time, the leader can seek out qualitative data from people in the know like parents, teachers, and district employees.

Part 3—Performance Diagnostic Checklist. These questions help you diagnose the reason behind any performance gap linked to Parts 1 and 2. Often, leaders are aware there is a problem, but they are not sure how to approach it. Moreover, some leaders try to fix different problems using the same approach. This can result in disaster when it comes to performance issues!

The questions in the Performance Diagnostic Checklist (PDC) originated from the work of Dr. John Austin (Austin, 2000), who created the tool for diagnosing performance issues. The PDC shown in *Quick Wins* is adapted from the original, modified for use by school leaders. The PDC is an interview-based assessment methodology covering four performance areas that often are at the root of a performance gap.

These areas are:

Antecedents and Information (these either set the stage or are "triggers" for peoples' behavior). Examples include policies and procedures, job aides, teacher evaluation guidelines, academic and daily schedules, training, announcements, etc.

Equipment and Processes (the tools, technology, and procedures in place to support behavior). Examples include computers, school supplies for students and teachers, walking path signage, etc.

Knowledge and Skills – Training (the specific knowledge and skills needed perform the behavior). Examples include teacher in-service training, teacher and student evaluation categories, and district personnel instructional coaching and mentoring.

Motivation (originally titled "Consequences," these are the outcomes of performing the behavior—what the individual experiences as a result). Examples include praise to teachers and students in the hallways, public recognition for academic achievement, and disciplinary action for misbehavior or violating school policy (for students, this might mean suspension; for educators, it might mean disciplinary action for violating the code of ethics).

Generally, the PDC is used by administrators with employees—specifically, subject matter experts (SMEs) who can provide enough depth for analyzing the performance gap. In large systems, or districts with multiple sites, it can be delivered using a sampling approach (e.g., selecting a couple of teachers from each grade level) to avoid taking a great deal of time.

The PDC can and should be used in conjunction with direct observations to support the validity of the results. It is because of this last point that we recommend using the PDC only *following* completion of Parts 1 and 2 of **QuickWOC**. At this point, the school leaders have conducted their walkabouts, gathered additional insight from other support professionals, and can now diagnose the problem at hand before implementing the *Quick Win*.

To use the PDC, specify a behavior you are interested in seeing improve, based on Parts 1 and 2 of **QuickWOC**. Be specific. Then, walk through the 20 PDC questions from the point of view of *who would be performing the behavior (staff, parent, student)*. For any "no" response, work with your team to identify the solution to address the gap. The solution is in fact the *Quick Win*.

Quick Wins

QuickWOC Part 1— Walkabout Observations

Use this scoring rubric:					
1	2	3	4	5	
Never	Rarely	Sometimes	Often	Always	
A. Arrival/Dismissal					**Score**
1. Students walk (not run) during transitions.					
2. Students follow communication expectations. (e.g., they speaking at a conversational level).					
3. Students follow a designated route.					
4. Students transition directly to the designated area per the school's expectations.					
5. Staff attend their post on time.					
6. Staff stand in assigned areas.					
7. Staff greet the students and interact with them in a positive manner.					
8. Staff consistently correct misbehavior.					
9. When correcting misbehavior, staff use a calm and respectful manner.					
10. When a student runs, staff require the student to walk back to where they began running.					
11. Students able to transition safely to their transportation.					
12. Students move on and off the sidewalk in an orderly manner.					
13. Students have designated areas to sit or stand safely when waiting for transportation.					
14. The front office staff smile at parents, students, and visitors when they enter the front office.					
15. The front office staff greet parents, students, and visitors. For example, "Good morning," "We'll be right with you."					
16. When answering the phone, the front office staff communicate in ways that convey respect, kindness, and an "at your service" attitude.					

Use this scoring rubric:				
1	2	3	4	5
Never	Rarely	Sometimes	Often	Always

	B. Hallways	Score
1.	Students walk (not run) during transitions.	
2.	Students follow communication expectations. (e.g., they speaking at a conversational level, not yelling).	
3.	Students follow a designated route.	
4.	Students transition directly to the designated area per the school's expectations.	
5.	Staff attend their post on time.	
6.	Staff stand in assigned areas.	
7.	Staff constantly monitor their assigned area.	
8.	Staff greet the students or provide random positive attention.	
9.	Staff consistently correct misbehavior.	
10.	When correcting misbehavior, staff use a calm and respectful manner.	
11.	When a student runs, staff require the student to walk back to where they began running.	

Quick Wins

Use this scoring rubric:				
1	**2**	**3**	**4**	**5**
Never	**Rarely**	**Sometimes**	**Often**	**Always**

C. Cafeteria	Score
1. Students transition through the line efficiently.	
2. It is easy for students to find seating (the process of finding a seat creates little to no tension among students).	
3. Students pick up trash and deposit it in the correct containers.	
4. Students follow expectations when they have finished eating.	
5. Students face forward with their feet on the ground.	
6. Students talk only to the students at their table and do not yell across tables.	
7. Students ask permission or follow school expectations before leaving their seat or area.	
8. Staff stand at assigned posts.	
9. Staff actively scan their assigned areas.	
10. Staff track potential problems and intervene early.	
11. Staff greet the students and interact with them in a positive manner.	
12. Staff consistently correct misbehaviors like students leaving their area without permission or yelling across tables.	
13. Staff provide more positive interactions than corrections.	
14. Staff follow through on warnings for repeated misbehavior.	
15. Staff refrain from grouping and speaking amongst themselves.	

Use this scoring rubric:				
1	2	3	4	5
Never	Rarely	Sometimes	Often	Always

D. Playground/Fields	Score
1. There are clearly identified boundaries.	
2. The equipment is organized and easy to access.	
3. Students use the playground equipment safely.	
4. The equipment is clean and safe.	
5. Staff consistently monitor students.	
6. Staff refrain from grouping and speaking among themselves.	
7. Staff actively scan their assigned areas.	
8. Staff track potential problems and intervene early.	

Use this scoring rubric:				
1	2	3	4	5
Never	Rarely	Sometimes	Often	Always

E. Bathrooms	Score
1. There are clearly identified boundaries.	
2. Students enter the bathrooms in reasonable numbers (i.e. not too many students in the bathroom at one time).	
3. Students use the facility for its intended purpose.	
4. Bathroom areas have procedures that ensure students will not congregate.	
5. Staff monitor the bathroom areas to check for safety and cleanliness.	

Use this scoring rubric:				
1	2	3	4	5
Never	Rarely	Sometimes	Often	Always

F. Classrooms	Score
1. Students respond in a well-behaved manner toward the teacher and other adults in the room.	
2. Students respect the materials and property in the classroom.	
3. Students respect their fellow students.	
4. Core subject areas receive uninterrupted blocks of time.	
5. Classrooms have established routines and procedures that include behavioral expectations for all activities and transitions.	

Use this scoring rubric:				
1	2	3	4	5
Never	Rarely	Sometimes	Often	Always

G. Facilities	Score
1. The school façade or the school grounds appear to be in good condition.	
2. The inside of the building, including bathrooms, hallways, storage areas, and teacher workrooms in good condition.	
3. Classrooms have enough storage cabinets, etc. to maintain a clean and orderly environment for learning?	
4. Students and teachers access materials easily and quickly.	

QuickWOC Part 2— Other Sources

Additional Sources of Information	Observation Notes
Staff 1. What are changes that could be made easily and quickly, which would make a difference to staff in doing their daily work? 2. Are there materials and/or resources that staff need?	
Parents 3. What areas do parents feel the need to change quickly to improve the school environment and help their children learn?	
Community 4. Are there changes that could occur quickly and that would make a difference to the community and its perception of the school?	
Observation Team 5. What are the most pervasive problems identified by the team? 6. How do the observations of the team align with comments from staff, parents, and the community? **Of these problems, which ones could be most easily remedied?**	

QuickWOC Part 3— Performance Diagnostic Checklist

Specify a behavior you need to improve, based on Parts 1 and 2 of *QuickWOC*. Walk through the questions from the viewpoint of *the* person performing the behavior. For any "No" response, identify a solution, the solution may in fact be a *Quick Win*.

Antecedents and Information	YES	NO
1. Is there a written description telling *exactly* what is expected of the educator regarding a particular instructional/behavioral/behavioral strategy?		
2. Has the educator received adequate instruction about what to do (e.g., instructions like "I want you to do this and this before we leave today")?		
3. Has the educator received formal training on this instructional/behavioral strategy? If yes, check all applicable training methods? [ ] Instructions [ ] Demonstration [ ] Rehearsal [ ]		
4. Are there task aids visible **while** completing the instructional/behavioral strategy in question (e.g., reminders to prompt the strategy in the correct way at the correct time/duration)?		
5. Can the educator state the purpose of the instructional/behavioral strategy?		
6. Is the educator ever verbally, textually, or electronically reminded to use the instructional/behavioral strategy? If yes, how often? Hourly [ ] Daily [ ] Weekly [ ] Monthly [ ] By who? Check all that apply: Peer [ ] Coach [ ] Administrator [ ] Other [ ]		

Quick Wins

Antecedents and Information	YES	NO
7. Are there frequently updated, challenging, and attainable goals the educator is comfortable with in relation to the instructional/behavioral strategy?		
8. Is the educator "aware" of the mission of the school?		
Equipment and Processes	YES	NO
9. If equipment is required, is it available and in good working order (e.g. computer, A/V, mic, etc.)?		
10. Is the equipment and environment optimally arranged in a physical sense (e.g., the arrangement of the students' desks)?		
11. Are larger processes performing well despite any incorrect instructional/behavioral strategies along the way (e.g. routines and procedures)?		
12. Are these processes written out and arranged in a logical manner?		
13. Are teachers able to implement the instructional/behavioral strategy without any obstacles (e.g. interruption by the intercom)?		
Knowledge and Skills—Training	YES	NO
14. Can the educator tell you what he/she is supposed to be doing and how to do it?		
15. Can the educator physically/verbally precisely demonstrate the instructional/behavioral strategy?		
16. If the instructional/behavioral strategy needs to be completed quickly, can the educator perform it at the appropriate speed?		

Quick Wins

Motivation	YES	NO
17. Are employees motivated based on the outcomes following completion of the task?		
18. Do educators see the positive effects of implementing the instructional/behavioral strategy (e.g. increased student engagement, increased assessment data, decreased misbehavior)?		
19. Do administrators monitor the educator? If yes, how often? Hourly [ ] Daily [ ] Weekly [ ] Monthly [ ]		
20. Does the educator receive feedback about the performance? If yes, By whom? _____ and How often? _____ How long of a delay is the feedback delivered from the instructional/behavioral strategy? _____ Check all that apply? Feedback Focus: Positive [ ] Constructive [ ] Feedback Type: Written [ ] Verbal [ ] Graphed [ ] Other [ ]		
21. Is the instructional/behavioral strategy easy to implement?		
22. Do other instructional/behavioral strategies appear to take precedence over the targeted strategy?		

Chapter 4: Quick Wins Need S.M.A.R.T. Goals and Data

Once you've determined which *Quick Wins* you will target for change, set goals. Goals give leaders and school staff a clear destination and let you adjust course as needed. We use *S.M.A.R.T. goals:*

S.M.A.R.T. goals are

Specific, Motivational, Achievable,

Relevant, and Trackable

S.M.A.R.T. goals are popular and highly effective among practitioners of Organizational Behavior Management, or OBM *(Geller, 2003)*. They are an efficient and memorable way to get results.

S.M.A.R.T. Goals

S.M.A.R.T. goals are Specific, Motivational, Achievable, Relevant, and Trackable. Here is a look at each element:

Specific—the goal is stated in clear, unambiguous words. A specific goal has a much greater chance of being accomplished because it describes precisely what you are looking to change, and what behaviors must occur to achieve it. To illustrate, a general goal would be "get in shape," but a specific S.M.A.R.T. goal would be "join a health club, work out three days a week, and track the exercises you complete and how long you work out."

Motivational—the goal motivates by stating why the change is important, how feedback will be provided on performance, and how goal achievement will be celebrated. We are not talking about intrinsic motivation, where people are energized simply by the nature of the goal. We are talking about *actions leaders take* to motivate people to engage in the change.

Achievable—the goal is clearly linked to what employees must demonstrate to achieve the goal, and the resources to be provided.

Relevant—the goal is something people can relate to from the start—part of day-to-day work, clearly linked to roles and responsibilities, with the change clearly adding value for those affected by the change.

Trackable—the goal clearly states how it will be measured, tracked, and ultimately how progress and achievement will be determined.

An Example of *S.M.A.R.T.* in Action

A school wanted to help employees and assistant principals to be more competent in evaluating performance and developing their careers. This was important because there were new personnel and use of contractors had grown from previous years. The school implemented a new performance management system for staff, faculty, and contractors that used clearly defined processes and guidelines. The new system was reviewed monthly and all personnel were provided feedback monthly on their efforts and the results.

The goal was to have each employee and administrator use the new performance management system to develop specific career plans and evaluate performance on their respective roles and responsibilities (***Specific***) because there were new personnel and use of contractors had grown from previous years (***Motivational***). Also the new system would provide all personnel with feedback on their efforts and the results of the process (***Motivational***). During feedback discussions, employees would have the opportunity to describe to school leaders if resources were adequate or more resources would be needed (***Achievable***). Personnel would have access to the system as part of their day-to-day operations, and would be the basis of their own performance reviews (***Relevant***). The school leadership would monitor the use of the new system, track usage and completion of performance reviews and career plans, and collect data on the impact to the school's overall performance (***Trackable***).

It has been our experience that using a set of questions to guide the development of S.M.A.R.T. goals provides an efficient, practical, and focused method for developing achievable goals.

Data, Data, Data!

After identifying your SMART goals, it's essential to use data to manage and celebrate *Quick Wins*.

Using data does not have to be complicated. You can—and should—create your own way of measuring your *Quick Wins*. You might be thinking, "I don't have time or the knowledge for creating metrics." That's understandable, given advancements in technology and complicated, expensive measurement systems. Many marvel at the ability of these systems, but frequently lack the money to purchase them or the patience and desire to learn how to use them efficiently.

Most schools have some sort of data measures for counting something—number of students, grades, attendance, teacher vacation days, turnover, tenure, and budgets for example. However, if the school or district doesn't have the data needed, you can create *your own* "scoreboard" to illustrate progress on a select few S.M.A.R.T. Goals. The process of selecting and creating your own data measures should be simple once you've walked through the development of your S.M.A.R.T. Goals.

S.M.A.R.T. Questions to Ask

To help you develop S.M.A.R.T. goals, we offer a set of questions. Use these questions to help think through how the change will happen, discussing with the dedicated team, including those who are affected by the change. Include the team dedicated to making the change happen, and those affected by the change.

Specific

- *Precisely what are you attempting to change at your school?* Clearly and concisely answer in words that will be easily be understood by those who need to engage in the change. One way to make sure of your precision is to consider a new employee. A new teacher joins the school, and she needs to understand how to perform various tasks throughout the day. Precision can be the very differentiator between a smooth and quick onboarding, versus a long drawn out training effort.
- *What behaviors must occur to achieve the desired outcome?* Clearly state who must do what, when, and how.

Motivational

- *Why should people engage in the change?* Address the potential benefit and impact to the school, staff, and/or students.
- *How will feedback be provided?* Planned feedback will be key to create momentum on the change. (We will address feedback more in depth shortly.)
- *How will we celebrate success of the Quick Win?* Taking time to acknowledge the end result is just as important as implementing the change.

Quick Wins

Achievable
- *Do staff have the knowledge and skills to reach this goal?*
- *Are short-term goals (targets) established for the Quick Win?*
- *Are resources provided to support those who need to implement or engage in the change (time, tools, money, authority, etc.)?*

Relevant
- *Is the goal part of the day-to-day duties of those who will need to change?*
- *Is the change clearly laid out in the roles and responsibilities of those who will need to change?*
- *Is making this change adding value for the students, teachers, and/or staff?*

Trackable
- *How will you determine progress and achievement for this goal?*
- *Does your school employ database systems to reinforce progress toward school academic and climate goals?*
- *Does your school have ongoing measures for climate and student/teacher efficacy?*

Examples: Using SMART Goals and *QuickWOCs*

Dirty, Dingy Hallways

QuickWOC **Assessment and Rationale:** Ten dirty, dingy hallways and school entrance need painting—could give parents and students impression that staff are not "invested" in school.

S.M.A.R.T. Goal: Schedule maintenance to paint 10 hallways and entrance prior to the return of students and staff to improve the hallways appearance. A non-specific goal might just say "paint the hallways."

Data Measures and Feedback: Use checklist for 10 hallways and entrance. All stakeholders can see changes themselves, and school leaders will provide feedback to staff.

Unapproachable Administration

QuickWOC **Assessment and Rationale:** A year-end climate survey reveals that staff perceive administration to be unapproachable and not "hearing" or acting on their needs. Administration understands the need for staff buy-in to meet future goals, motivating them to change that perception.

S.M.A.R.T. Goal: Use 3+3+60=Trust strategy (in later chapter) in the first staff meeting to identify and act on top 3 needs.

Data Measures and Feedback: Conduct the same climate survey after 30 and 60 days to assess staff perception.

Develop measures for each SMART Goal. Give staff weekly feedback on progress toward goals.

Morning Fights

***QuickWOC* Assessment and Rationale:** Discipline data indicate frequent morning fights in cafeteria. Staff interviews reveal no existing expectations for students or staff.

S.M.A.R.T. Goal: Develop cafeteria procedures at first discipline team meeting. Then train cafeteria staff in these procedures on the first in-service day.

A non-achievable goal might be to require more staff in the cafeteria in a school that already has staff issues.

Data Measures and Feedback: Use sign-in sheets for training.

Collect discipline data at end of 2 weeks to measure student behavior. During first week, directly observe each staff with checklist of key behaviors (supervise area, provide praise to students, give students time-out for misbehavior).

Long Lines

***QuickWOC* Assessment and Rationale:** Lunch staff complains of long lines and students complain they lack time to eat lunch. Two students return to class highly irritable. Directly observing arrival of classes at cafeteria discloses that 16 of 20 classes were not punctual. Discover that teachers' clocks are not synchronized across school.

S.M.A.R.T. Goal: Immediately schedule maintenance to synchronize clocks. Send email to solicit feedback on any existing barriers to punctuality. Share finalized schedule with staff. Give raffle ticket to teachers who arrive within a 2-minute window.

While easy to track staff arrival after syncing clocks, collecting baseline data prior to intervention allows for tracking and reinforcement of improvements.

Data Measures and Feedback: Use existing schedule to mark arrival of classes on time.

Give teacher a raffle ticket and thank them for arriving on time.

Email staff noting any improvements in punctuality (e. g. "We've gone from 20% punctuality to 80% in just one day. You guys are the best!!").

Email all staff noting improvements during lunchtime resulting from changes.

SMART Goals in Action

When it comes to SMART goals, here are five important things to consider. Each can potentially make or break your turnaround:

1. What do you want people to do more of, less of, or differently?

2. What measures will indicate movement, telling you the turnaround is working? What "leading indicators" will tell the story?

3. What tools will you use to collect data, and who will collect, report, and review it?

4. Once you've selected your measures, whom will you designate to create a simple "scoreboard" to share regularly with staff?

5. When you initiate change, we highly recommend presenting measures of progress to targeted staff at least weekly, no less than monthly.

Here is a look at each—

Consideration #1: What do you want people to do more of, less of, or differently? Determine the results you desire related to the school's ultimate goals, and define staff behaviors that align with these ultimate goals. It is important to be precise here.

For example, we once asked staff to focus more on students transitioning to class during morning arrival by standing at key places and providing "positive attention" to students as entered the school. However, during our first morning observation, we realized that our emphasis on "positive attention" inadvertently encouraged staff to ignore misbehavior: As students ran by, staff simply said "good morning"!

To remedy this, we had a five-minute meeting prior to school start the next day. We acknowledged our failure to be specific, and reminded staff to not only increase focus on positive interactions but consistently correct misbehavior as well. We modeled what positive interactions should look like, and then gave an example of the most common misbehavior at the time—running—and how to correct it.

(By the way, the correction was very simple. We asked staff to include one additional word when directing students to walk. That word was "back." If students began running, the directive was not just to say "walk," but "walk back" to where they began running. This quickly eliminated running in the halls!)

Consideration #2: What measures will indicate movement, telling you the turnaround is working? What "leading indicators" will tell the story? These can be measures like staff and student perception (e.g. climate surveys), staff and student attendance, staff timeliness to duties, counts of positive to negative interactions, and discipline data (Supovitz, Foley, & Mishook, 2012). Whatever data measures you select should tell the story of the turnaround—is it working? Are you moving toward the right result?

Consideration #3: What tools will you use to collect data, and who will collect, report, and review it? These tools may already be in place for data on discipline, attendance, student performance, etc. In the case of specific behaviors, a simple pencil-and-paper checklist can serve you well. For example, imagine asking one of your staff who is on duty during dismissal to simply tally how many students were running to the bus. Or ask an instructional coach to count how many times students called out during a whole-group instruction.

Remember, when we discuss behavior, we are not talking *only* about student behavior. You need to count teacher behavior as well. In the example of students calling out, a principal might count how many times a teacher used correction versus how many times praise was used.

While these measures are critical to a successful turnaround, they also can be critical for demonstrating to staff that the Quick Wins are working, and that the turnaround is happening in incremental steps versus waiting for an end result.

Consideration #4: Once you've selected your measures, whom will you designate to create a simple "scoreboard" to share regularly with staff? You might choose a designee for each measure. For example, discipline data might be shared by the school's psychologist, achievement data by the school's assistant principal, and student or teacher attendance data by the school's secretary. You can be creative in the data presentation and perhaps link it to your school theme. Make it fun! Data might be presented as multiple graphs posted in a weekly newsletter or common area where all staff can regularly view it. Or it can be posted on something that literally looks like a scoreboard. (More on graphic feedback later.)

Figure 2 is an example of how one school graphically showed the total number of "codes called in" (requests for assistance) to the administration (Gavoni, Edmonds, Gollery, & Kennedy, in press). Three codes described various behavior problems, and one indicated medical emergency. The data was collected and graphed to show teachers and administrators how the codes were being used to monitor behavior over time.

Codes Called in Cafeteria by Month

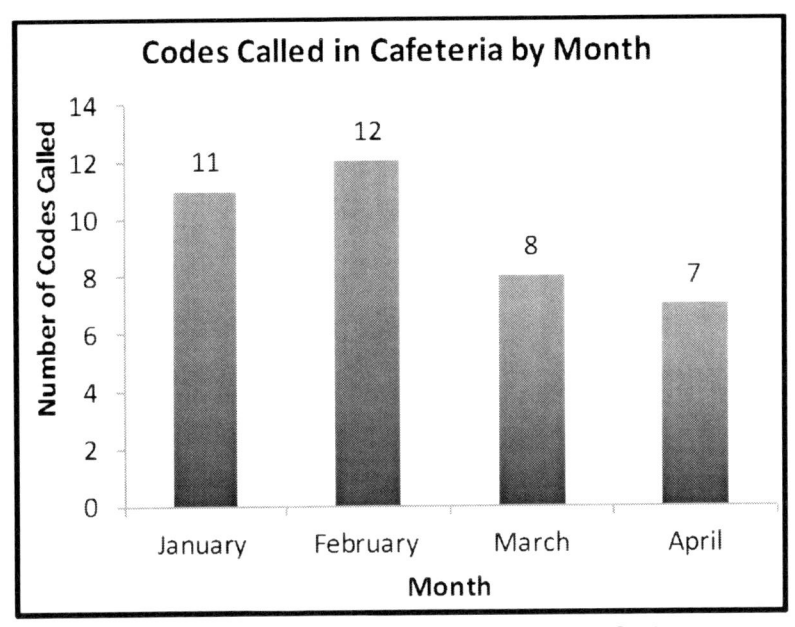

Month	Number of Codes Called
January	11
February	12
March	8
April	7

Figure 2. Codes called in cafeteria by month. (Codes were: 1 = continuous aggression and/or self-injury observed; 2 = continuous high-magnitude disruption and/or property disruption; 3 = student out of assigned area; blue = medical emergency.)

Whatever method you use, be sure to list three-to-five data measures with targets set on some timetable (weekly, monthly, quarterly). This gives the staff a visual of the data, and sets anticipation for looking for the updates to view progress toward the goals.

Consideration # 5: When you initiate change, we highly recommend presenting measures of progress to targeted staff at least weekly, no less than monthly. Just as a sports team needs to know the score and where they are on the field ASAP to reinforce or adjust plays, your school team needs to be fed back measures in a timely fashion.

For example, let's say that student discipline referrals are down 15% after one week, as a result of a new behavior support program. Teachers who are given this data are likely to feel empowered from seeing evidence of steady improvement. For another example, showing the leadership a staff absenteeism or a climate survey at the end of a month could demonstrate the impact of their support.

Once again, such data can be used to reinforce the current approach based on staffs' perceptions, or to adjust the current approach, or to communicate with the staff about any misperceptions that have been discovered through the data analysis.

> ## *Quick Wins* in Action:
> ## Involving Staff in Goal Selection

In many schools, goal-setting is approached as a top-down one-man show, but that has major drawbacks. Avoid simply imposing goals on people. If your staff does not feel involved, the process is already stalling. To create enthusiasm and commitment, involve your staff in goal-setting by seeking input from them. This can be done individually, and in small or large groups. Although the personal touch is always best, using surveys is an efficient strategy for gaining input in a way that allows you to easily recognize patterns. Involving your staff in selecting goals is one of your first *Quick Wins*.

We have had the good fortune to collaborate with John, a former turnaround principal and current assistant superintendent in a school district for the state of Florida. John's record as a principal includes an astounding four turnarounds! But here is what is even more amazing: one was with an elementary school, another with middle or junior high school, and the two most recent turnarounds were in larger high schools. Whatever John was doing, we need more of it!

We asked John how he put *Quick Wins* into action. Here is what he shared about gaining buy-in and trust as a *Quick Win*.

3 + 3 + 60 = Trust

In the first meeting with his new staff, John said, *"Give me 3 things you don't want me to change (keepers), and 3 things you do want me to change (fixes)."* And he did this in his first 60 minutes with them. What did it build? *Trust.* Thus the magic formula:

$$3+3+60 = Trust.$$

Some of the answers surprised John, but others not at all. The "keepers" gave great insight into what the staff deeply valued, such as customs, rituals, and celebrations held near and dear. As John would say, "Don't mess with these or you'll unsettle the masses." The "fixes" were things the staff perceived as needing immediate attention. Many were simple managerial behaviors, like being more visible around campus. Throughout the 60 minutes, the team charted all the responses and reached a consensus by listing "3 keepers and 3 fixes." John utilized the 3+3+60 to initiate *Quick Wins* that turned around three underperforming schools within seven years. (Note: when you employ the 3+3+60 = Trust, you only get one shot at it, at the very beginning of the relationship. If you get it right, everyone wins huge benefits!)

By devoting his time to the fixes, the staff immediately began to trust John, as he was attentive to their stated needs. The "fixes" were taking place while John simultaneously celebrated the "keepers," and in doing so, established that he valued what his team held as being important for *them* and *their* school. *Their voices* were heard, and the new guy wasn't barging in to change and/or invalidate everything they had. If you use the 3+3+60 = trust strategy, make sure you spend the first semester 100% committed to addressing the six items, while constantly scanning the landscape for additional Quick Wins. And don't move in on the big ones yet! If you implement this simple 3+3+60 strategy just right, in your staff's eyes you will likely become the best thing since spring break. You will be accepted, you will have earned their trust, and now any big changes you want to implement in the second semester or Year Two will be easier mountains to climb.

Chapter 5: Quick Wins Require Communication

"And words are, of course, the most powerful drug used by humankind."

Thus spoke author Rudyard Kipling in his 1923 address to the Royal College of Surgeons in London.

The capacity of communication to make or break any change cannot be overstated. The old saying, "sticks and stones may break my bones, but words will never hurt me," rings hollow within school hallways. Words *do* have the power to break morale, effort, momentum, relationships, and ultimately achievement. *What, when, and how* a leader communicates is the *most powerful tool* that can be used to *make or break* a school.

When used positively, words have the ability to motivate, strengthen, and build a school that can positively impact generations of families. And positively impact the world, because of the fundamental importance of education to the lives of students and civil societies.

Effective communication is essential for all leaders who seek to bring out the best in their staff within any organization. In schools, communication represents the absolute core of strengthening relationships, improving performance, and fostering self-efficacy in ways that help students achieve. Given the unequivocal power of communication, it is a shame that more educational leadership preparation programs do not provide greater focus in this area.

Communication is very complex, as it entails a combination of body language, tone of voice, timing, and content. Even with the complexities of communication, there are simple strategies that, when used at the right time and in the right way, can have a profound, positive, and lasting effect on staff behavior and morale. There are things a leader can say, as well as things a leader cannot "unsay."

School leaders must be aware that their communication is under constant scrutiny. Each time a leader effectively communicates, it is comparable to making a deposit in what we call the "relationship bank." However, each time a leader is ineffective in communication, it is like making a withdrawal. And what happens when you withdraw more money than you've deposited in your bank? Overdraft fees!

In the context of school improvement, "overdraft fees" can manifest in a "negative balance" that includes lack of motivation, reduced trust in administration, and development of a negative climate. While certain well-timed communication strategies can lead to significant deposits, it only takes one poorly timed, ineffective attempt to communicate to stall a turnaround, or even sink it for good.

The turnaround process is a fragile endeavor and communication blunders during the early stages can have a negative effect that is multiplied. We've seen well-meaning leaders err during the critical launch, never to recover. Staff quickly lose faith in such a leader and quickly begin to mistrust and dislike the person.

(Warning! If your staff does not like you, your attempts at communication will likely lose the desired impact. In fact, even strategies like praise will not be positively received.)

Our relationship-bank analogy is affirmed by Aubrey Daniels (2000) when he emphatically states, "to make reinforcement, reward, and recognition effective, you must first develop good relationships with people."

Seven Communication Strategies for Quick Wins

Do you struggle with communicating or developing relationships? If so, or if you just want to improve your communication in a way that further strengthens relationships, try the following communication strategies. These help build leaders who are effective communicators—well-liked and inspiring staff to go above and beyond.

These communication strategies foster collective self-efficacy and create a phenomenon called "positive emotional contagion" (Kramer et al., 2014). It is characterized by the spreading of contented staff perception and the optimistic feeling and productive behaviors that typify contented people. We categorize these communication strategies as *Quick Wins,* because they are!

Communication *Quick Win* #1— The Power of Persuasion

As a school leader, your position enables you to leverage the power of persuasion. With the knowhow to persuade through effective communication, you can forge relationships essential to ensuring that *Quick Wins* are implemented. In *From Good Schools to Great Schools: What Their Principals Do Well,* authors Gray and Streshly provide a comprehensive comparison of principals and corporate leaders, including qualities exclusive to school leadership. The authors eloquently share how "school leaders matter because they have the clout to mold the conversation, the topic, and how the topic is talked about" (Gray & Streshly, 2008, p. 15).

School leaders have the influence to bring people within a school together and shape the culture. This is not to be confused with simply telling folks what to do. The idea is to provide a framework of collaboration to shape a community toward caring and mutual learning that permeates throughout the school. This learning occurs through two primary sources: positive and constructive feedback. Positive feedback is specific information intended to reinforce teacher or staff behavior by letting he or she know exactly what they are doing correctly. Constructive feedback is specific information intended to help the teacher or staff do something more, less, or differently. Both types of feedback are intended to help people in regards to performance goals.

**Communication *Quick Win* #2—
Performance-Based Feedback**

The power of feedback to unlock the best performance is critical, and often overlooked or underutilized. Performance feedback provides information that guides behavior in the right direction—from debating to making decisions, from fighting fires to strategic planning, from directing to effective teaching. Feedback encourages the correct behavior to happen. Without it, people would be guessing at how they are doing, what they are doing, and in the worst case, thinking they are doing all the right things when in reality, they may be doing all the wrong things. *In turnaround schools, feedback is the single most valuable behavior leaders can engage in for improving staff performance.* The goal of performance feedback is simple: help people perform to achieve results. By increasing or adding more performance-based feedback, leaders can immediately unlock a *Quick Win* toward accelerating and achieving performance goals during a turnaround.

For example, at one turnaround school, behavioral issues that once plagued the hallways had been reduced to only minor issues. However, student achievement was still stagnated. Some were calling it a "Happy-Crappy" school. After doing a walkabout and noting limited engagement, leaders determined that what would have the largest impact on achievement would be to increase student engagement. Specifically, this meant helping teachers engage their students by asking higher-order thinking questions at an increased rate.

After providing a brief in-service on a managing-response-rate technique (e.g., choral responding during whole-group activities), the principal would prompt use of the response-rate technique. At the beginning of each day prior to students arriving, she used the school's intercom to wish all staff a "good morning," and then reminded the teachers of the managing-response-rate strategy to focus on during the week. By doing this, teachers knew what the leadership team would be looking for as they walked through classrooms. Moreover, the leadership team knew what to provide feedback on. As the leadership team walked through, they made quick notes regarding exactly what teachers were doing well, and what slight changes would help them further improve. At the end of the day leadership put out an email highlighting exceptional managing-response rate techniques observed, praised staff for their efforts, and then provided tips on how to further improve for those who were trying, but still not implementing with fidelity. Leadership then repeated the process until almost all were performing the technique with precision, and then celebrated success as student achievement began to grow.

Communication *Quick Win* #3—
Sub-Goals

In Organizational Behavior Management (OBM), a fundamental premise to achieve performance is the effective use of sub-goals. By reinforcing progress toward sub-goals, the path to achieving the ultimate end goal remains clear. Leaders can establish a *Quick Win* by setting frequent sub-goals followed by frequent performance feedback and reinforcement. If the leader has targeted the right behaviors to reinforce, results are all but instantaneous.

It is not unusual for sub-goals to be viewed as small changes, and for most of the "small changes" to simply go unnoticed. By focusing on sub-goals, the leader has implemented a communication *Quick Win*, enabling the leader to look for and reinforce those "small changes." It is a key role of leadership to illuminate even the smallest improvement during a school turnaround, and provide feedback that aligns performance directly with it.

In the example of the managing-response-rate strategy illustrated above, a first sub-goal might be to have at least 20% of teachers observed trying out the strategy. The next sub-goal would be increased to 40%, and so on.

Communication *Quick Win* #4— Feedback Develops Self-Efficacy

Instructional self-efficacy is a teacher's belief in his or her capacity to effectively instruct. It has been demonstrated to be a large predictor of teacher and student success (Bandura, 1977, 1986, 1997). Self-efficacy reflects confidence in the teacher's ability to exert control over their own motivation, behavior, and social environment. Self-efficacy is not built magically. Evidence of success is needed to build self-efficacy and collective efficacy within a school, and feedback is *the* essential element required for building efficacy.

By focusing on feedback to develop self-efficacy, a leader is implementing a *Quick Win* that will last. When people value doing something and believe they can do it, they have the ingredients required for success. As your staff accumulates successful experiences, their self-efficacy grows.

As leader, it is your job to provide as much feedback as possible toward incremental improvement in their performance. However, it is not just about providing feedback, but providing feedback *strategically*. Seek to provide information that allows your staff to see where they stand against their own personal goals, not the goals or performance of others.

By focusing your feedback on a student's or teacher's performance related to their goals, *and* delivering that feedback in a way that influences improvement, you are engaging the individual's confidence to perform—their self-efficacy.

> # Communication *Quick Win* #5—
> ## Feedback Strengthens Relationships

Leaders can use feedback to strengthen relationships with their teams. During turnarounds, leaders need to make every attempt to catch people doing things right. This triggers leaders to give positive feedback up to four times as often as they give constructive feedback. Why?

Imagine a school where, every time a teacher or student saw you, they turned around and walked the other way. The moment they see you, it triggers an emotional response—"Oh, it's him, better go the other way."

During school turnarounds, the health of relationships is critical to success. This may sound "fluffy" or "soft," but consider the results you are achieving under the conditions during the turnaround—people are already on edge, feeling emotions like helplessness, being concerned, and possible fear for their jobs. You need to actively build and strengthen relationships with the team. Providing feedback, especially positive feedback, is a great way to do so.

> **Communication *Quick Win* #6—
> Constructive Feedback for
> Helping People Improve**

It is not unusual for leaders to avoid confrontation. When this happens, they tend to allow subpar performance to occur, even in their presence. In school turnarounds, the contrary may be true—when leaders deliver more constructive feedback, it helps to make the right things happen.

The problem is that this level and delivery of constructive feedback is, well, not constructive. It is negative, potentially damaging, and possibly hindering performance. You can deliver constructive feedback as a *Quick Win* to accelerating performance, but it is important to understand key elements in delivering truly constructive feedback.

Doing nothing is doing something. By not correcting performance, it is virtually condoning it! Imagine a student jogging down the hallways, passing multiple staff, as he rushes to the cafeteria for lunch. Now, assuming the hallway rules require students to walk, staffs' failure to correct the behavior is likely to be seen as a go-ahead to jog. In fact, other students may soon believe that jogging in the hallways to lunch is acceptable behavior, and the next thing you know, the hallways feel like a track meet! (Doing *nothing* is doing *something*.)

The same goes for staff. We were in the cafeteria once and noticed lots of negative interaction as the monitoring staff constantly reprimanded students for speaking too loudly. The principal was present. The behavior management system in place required the staff to interact with students positively four times as often as they corrected misbehavior, but in this case, the interactions were closer to one positive to every 10 negative. The principal never provided feedback to the staff. Her presence and failure to provide feedback *silently condoned the staffs' behavior—and the students'*. (Doing *nothing* is doing *something*.)

Help not harm. Corrective feedback should be constructive by nature, with the intention of helping the person perform better, and not used as a means of confrontation or punishment. By delivering positive feedback four times more often than constructive feedback (what we call the *4:1 rule*), your constructive feedback will be better received, more productive, and change can be observed to occur almost immediately. However, if you address their behavior when it fails to meet goals more than you recognize improvement, your communication may rapidly descend into the very confrontation most people want to avoid.

In the example above, what might happen if the principal recognized each staff in the cafeteria when they provided a positive interaction to the students? Behavioral science tells us there is a very good chance that these folks will begin providing more positive interaction to students.

However, when the principal fails to recognize any growth in staff, and instead focuses on what they are not doing, pretty soon staff are likely to become unhappy, and will even seek to avoid the principal.

Deliver feedback in private. When providing corrective or constructive feedback, it is almost always best to do so privately. Nobody wants to be called out in public. Correcting performance in private shows staff respect, and makes it more likely they will hear what you have to say, as opposed to focusing on any embarrassment they feel in the moment.

Focus on the goal. Constructive feedback is about helping people. One sure way to do so is to focus on the goal. By reminding the individual of the goal, stating where their performance is in relation to the goal, and then giving them information to help them move toward that goal, success is more likely—faster, and with better quality.

If you were helping a sprinter improve track time, you wouldn't get far if you just said, "improve your time." Instead, let them know their time in relation to the goal ("Your goal is 52 seconds; you ran that 400 in 60), and then give them information to move them closer to that goal ("Don't forget to lengthen your stride off the turn.").

Focusing on the goal gives you a double: it depersonalizes the feedback while providing information to help them perform better.

Communication *Quick Win* #7— Graphic Feedback Strengthens Belief

If you have ever invested money in the stock market, and watched the Dow Jones graph steadily rise, it probably triggers a smile or two. Watching the graph rise gave you positive feedback, reinforcing your behavior to invest more, and strengthening your self-efficacy (i.e., you believe yourself capable of accurately selecting profitable stocks). Nobody had to pat you on the back, tell you what a great job you did, or roll out a red carpet. Simply watching that little line move in a favorable trajectory gave you the feedback needed to maintain your course and strengthen your confidence, encouraging more and maybe riskier investments that might have big returns.

Graphs can be shared to show more than results. They can and should be shared as performance feedback, highlighting collective behaviors that led to the desired results. Remember, the ultimate goal of performance feedback is to help your staff grow in targeted skills. By aligning changes in targeted behaviors (e.g., using a new managing-response-rate technique) with improvement in meaningful results (like increased student engagement, decreased disruptions, increased academic achievement), even staff who are slow to engage in an initiative will take note and embrace the change. All of this can occur through using timely, targeted graphic feedback of group data.

A word of caution. A principal once caught wind of how we were using staff performance and results graphs. Feeling a need for change, she promptly had her leadership team do a walkthrough to collect data on a strategy her teachers were "trained" to use two months prior in their daily instruction. Once all data were collected, she posted it along with the results: Less than 5% of the teachers were actually using the strategy!

As you can imagine, the teacher union was inundated with complaints to the school, and the principal was promptly (and incorrectly in our opinion) reprimanded by union representatives. Did this make her a bad principal? Absolutely not! It was her intention to motivate staff through the use of these metrics. However, she missed out on a couple of important things. The first was to collect baseline data, completing observations prior to the training to see where performance pre-training. Since the teachers had been trained two months before, that initial walkthrough where only 5% of the staff were performing the skill could have been kept as the baseline. You have to know where you are (baseline) before you can move toward where you want to be (your goal).

Second, the principal should have informed the teachers of the leadership focus on collecting data on the new targeted behavior. The knowledge of the leader's commitment would serve as a trigger to the staff. They would know what the leadership would be looking for and reinforcing. To achieve the goal, people need to know what is expected and anticipate what will be reinforced.

Let's revisit the informing of staff about a leader's intent to observe and collect data. Some argue that the act of informing will cause behavior to happen, regardless of observations and collecting data. And this is absolutely correct. When employees know that leaders are going to show up, take data, give them feedback, and provide reinforcement, thiis will indeed make behavior happen. In fact, during turnarounds, this approach has never failed—every time staff was informed, behavior happened! Is that a bad thing? No, of course not, that's the point. The goal is to get the staff to try the skills in a way that provides ample reinforcement. By demonstrating the skills, leaders have but one thing to do—provide positive reinforcement. If the principal would have done this, they would have had baseline data, and the newly collected data. Even if the improvement is not vast, the leader still is in position to reinforce the improvement. A simple picture or graph in an email with a brief note saying, "I'm proud of you! We are moving in the right direction!" can be enough to reinforce performance. Incidentally, when it comes to publicly shared graphed data, the focus should not be on the behavior of individuals but rather on the performance or results of a group (e.g. whole school, grade group)? Individual data is almost always best to share in private, *especially* when it is data that indicates poor performance or results.

This process should be in every leader's toolkit during a turnaround, and repeat throughout the turnaround:
1. Specifically define behavior—What do you want people to do?
2. Get a baseline—discover where the performance is.
3. Observe and measure—take notes, find out if anything is getting in the way of performance, and take care of it.
4. Watch performance happen, and provide positive feedback.
5. Reinforce using graphic and verbal feedback until the skill is being performed at an acceptable level.

Graphic feedback is a simple and powerful tool for influencing behavior. Graphing progress is a very efficient and highly effective means of motivating staff. When goals are set, graphics help staff to easily discern where they are toward the goals. When educators value the goal and have sufficient self-efficacy to believe they can meet the goal, a graph provides strong reinforcement toward achieving the turnaround.

Chapter 6: Quick Wins Require Positive Leadership (Round 2)

A defining characteristic of successful organizations is leadership. Why people stay or leave organizations comes down to leadership. Not surprisingly, what makes *Quick Wins* successful during school turnarounds is active, proactive, engaging leadership.

Leadership is the process of influencing others (Vroom & Jago, 2007). Daniels and Daniels discern the true *Measure of a Leader* (2007) by looking at the behavior of those who are the leader's followers. But these general ways of describing leaders overlook one critical aspect: *leading others should be directed toward a positive outcome.*

Without this critical positive element in leadership, one could describe Hitler, Genghis Kahn, and Saddam Hussein as great leaders! Each influenced others and was followed by many. However, their leadership resulted in horrible acts of violence and oppression, ruling others without regard to consequences, and punishing those who defied them.

Such leadership has no place in business or education, and thus we use this definition:

Leadership is influencing others to achieve a positive outcome for them.

Characteristics of Positive Leadership

Several characteristics of positive leadership have been researched. In 2015, Krapfl and Kruja wrote for the *Journal of Organizational Behavior Management* a list of common leader characteristics that we find supportive for a successful school turnaround. We summarize nine of them here to provide content and links to the turnaround experience.

1. Leaders provide a value proposition: Similar to a vision, where the leader specifies a future state, a value proposition identifies the relationship between the organization and the larger context the organization serves. What is our value proposition as educators? It is to provide excellent education to produce the next generation of scientists, writers, businesspeople, and generally speaking, contributors to societies.

As Krapfl and Kruja (2015) share, when leading an organization in a new direction, "if the value proposition is not strong, the effort will ultimately fail." During a school turnaround, a leader can provide such a value proposition to the educators teaching the students, the parents of the students, and the external community. The school can turn around, and once the turnaround is complete, everyone wins. That's the value.

2. Leaders show ethical values: Leaders must be ethical. They must demonstrate high integrity to earn the trust of their followers. In the educational system, this is essential. Leaders who do not have the trust of their people can and will fail in the long run, regardless of *Quick Wins*. These ethical values create trust, create demand for success, and create long-term viability for the school.

3. Leaders demonstrate execution skills: Our focus on *Quick Wins* is about executing strategies that will make a positive impact to the school during a tough time. Unfortunately, there is an abundant challenge to this: execution typically is not taught in school, and skill in execution is often missing in leaders of organizations, whether business or educational.

Many leaders make the mistake of assuming that, once a plan is understood by everyone, implementation is simple. Nothing is further from the truth! Plans do not turn into actions automatically. They demand leadership to make things happen, engaging people to implement the plans to make a difference. Leaders can learn execution skills, and should learn from others, mentors, and formal higher education.

4. Leaders encourage innovation and creativity: An effective leader's role is to engage people to be innovative and creative, especially during a turnaround. Without innovation and creativity, morale can be low and results can stagnate or even be unachievable. For a new leader, this is a special challenge, because the staff has a history with the school and they might be resistant to the new leader's efforts.

5. Leaders demonstrate excellent communication skills: As previously illustrated, *Quick Wins* require communication. Leaders must be good communicators, from conveying the vision and strategy to using communication skills for coaching and feedback. Without solid communication skills, leaders can and will fail.

6. Leaders demonstrate enabling skills: This characteristic is about empowerment. By empowering people to make decisions, work together, and focus on critical needs, the turnaround process will be accelerated. Leaders can demonstrate enabling skills by setting expectations for decision-making, drawing clear lines of when and where the team can make decisions, and fundamentally providing the time and resources needed to enable performance to happen.

7. Leaders reinforce team-building skills: We cannot underestimate the power of the team during the turnaround process. This characteristic should actually be first on the list as during a turnaround, which requires "all hands on deck" to engage the team in working together to drive change. Leaders who reinforce team-building skills will accelerate the turnaround process.

8. *Leaders confront adversity*: Leaders do not avoid adversity. They confront it head on. Taking the time to understand why the adversity exists, what's at the root, and collaborating toward a solution can be the differentiator between success and failure. During the turnaround process, leaders will be faced with difficult goals, problems with people implementing the change, and even the magnitude of the change itself. At the end, leaders must be proactive, not reactive, to manage the change with minimal adversity.

9. *Leaders develop a culture*: Culture, simply defined, is "The way we do things around here." Culture can be decades old or newly minted. From the way administrators roam the school hallways, to break times for educators and staff, "how we do things around here" can take many forms. For leaders during a turnaround process, developing the right culture requires leadership to understand and define "How we *want* to do things around here.*"*

Quick Wins are critical to moving toward such a culture, but without a clear goal of what the culture looks like, the question then is "what kind of culture are we going to end up with?" By focusing on developing a culture, leaders can achieve great performance, long-lasting change, and a turnaround that stands the test of time.

From these nine characteristics, leaders can narrow their focus during the turnaround to achieve various *Quick Wins*.

Leadership Requirements to Achieve *Quick Wins*

There are three leadership requirements to achieve *Quick Wins:*

1. Quick Wins require leaders to *seek feedback*
2. Quick Wins require leaders to *be a positive stimulus*
3. Quick Wins require leaders to *implement a systematic feedback using a tiered approach:*

   Tier I— Learning new skills requires feedback

   Tier II—Feedback should be equitable, not equal

   Tier III—Performance management for ongoing success

Each is discussed in the following pages.

1. QUICK WINS—
Require leaders to seek feedback

During a turnaround, leaders (administrators, principals, teachers) are busy, nervous, and even fearful at times, given the often intense needs of the school. To achieve success in a turnaround environment, leaders must engage their team to achieve *Quick Wins*, and do so by demonstrating leadership that people will follow. Because so much is at stake, and so much is happening, leaders often wonder if they are doing all the right things.

Well, don't wonder: ask! By soliciting feedback from your team, you can get a clear pulse on how you are performing as a leader. Organizations around the world employ a variety of leadership feedback methods, such as feedback surveys and interviews, focus groups, and upward feedback reports. Such feedback is so common in business today that, in some cases, leaders receive more feedback than employees—which is not the ideal scenario. Even with this positive trend for business leaders to seek feedback, leadership feedback has only recently gained some ground in education.

By seeking feedback on your leadership behaviors during a turnaround, you are getting what could be the most critical data to achieve success—namely, information that allows you to determine how much are you helping or hurting the situation. Essentially, feedback on leadership behaviors provides an opportunity for the people around you—your employees, your peers, your supervisors—the opportunity to let you know how they think you are performing as a leader.

What you are looking for is patterns of common feedback from multiple sources. How you set expectations—are you confusing or clear? What your presence does to people—do they run or smile? How your feedback is received—is it harsh or helpful? This feedback on your leadership behavior will give you deep insight into how those around you perceive your leadership behaviors, and more importantly, the impact you are having on their performance, the school environment, and the probability of turnaround success. This data gives you the chance to change your behavior to support your people, support the school's performance, or make the turnaround that much more successful.

2. QUICK WINS—
Require leaders to be a positive stimulus

We can remember one time giving a presentation to a large group of teachers in the school's media center. The teachers were highly engaged. They were asking questions, making comments, smiling, and even laughing on occasion! But suddenly, things got very quiet. The questions stopped. No more comments. And you would think we were at a funeral, as not a smile was seen across the room. Laughter came to a screeching halt, like a bad joke in a comedy club.

What happened? It did not take long to determine the cause: the principal had entered through the side door. He walked in, scanned the room, looked at the presenter, and gave a nod to gesture "hello." He then sat in the chair nearest the door, suggesting that he might be leaving shortly, as he intermittently looked at his phone. His very presence changed everything. In short, this principal was not a positive stimulus.

How will you know if you are a positive stimulus during a turnaround? Ask yourself these questions:

> *How do my staff behave in my presence?*
> *How do my staff behave in my absence?*
> *What have I said or done when I've observed them performing well?*
> *What have I said or done when I've observed them performing poorly?*

Your answers will help you discover whether you are a positive or negative stimulus for your staff. Much like we observe a classroom and discern very quickly what behaviors have been targeted and reinforced by the teacher, we can observe the behaviors of the staff in the leader's presence and absence to quickly determine what key behaviors have been reinforced. As a leader, your behavior (or inaction) will have a tremendous impact on your staff's performance. Be aware of how staff behave in your presence.

During a turnaround, it is critical for leaders to be a positive stimulus for desired staff behavior. Think of yourself as the traffic light, and your staffs' behavior as the vehicle. What does your presence signal your staff to do? Does it tell them to interact positively with students, stand in a particular area in the cafeteria, or use a targeted instructional strategy they were recently trained on?

By setting performance goals and providing performance feedback as a norm, staff will be cued or "reminded" of these goals in your presence. When this happens, staff will at least attempt the targeted behavior, which gives you the opportunity to reinforce small changes, correct, or help them see the meaningful consequences of their behavior (e.g., increased engagement, decreased misbehavior, or improved achievement scores). When you target small goals and provide consistent deliberate feedback to staff, *just your presence* will evoke the performance you desire. You literally do not have to say a word, and your staff's behavior will change. *Sometimes doing nothing is doing something (Daniels, 2016)!*

What if no meaningful consequence occurred as a result of braking at the traffic light? Let's suspend disbelief for a moment, like we do at the movies. What if the traffic light were in the middle of nowhere, with no other cars in sight, no cop present, and you were in a rush? Would you stop? Some of us would, because of the guilt that might occur after years of operating under normal traffic rules. However, many of us would likely roll through the light . . . no harm done!

Sticking with the driving scenario, what if law enforcement *never* gave speeding tickets? Would you continue to double-check your speed or slow in their presence?

Or, let's reverse the strategy. What if, instead of giving drivers tickets for speeding, law enforcement intermittently pulled over law-abiding drivers and gave them a $100 discount on their insurance? How might that impact your behavior?

The point is, simply the presence of a traffic light or an officer has the power to *cue* certain behaviors when there are known consequences in place (ticket or reward). But when no consequences are in place (no ticket, no reward), what do you think would happen? There are just too many possibilities!

People tend to behave in ways that suit *them* best, which may not necessarily align with the law, or school rules, or your turnaround goals.

By focusing your leadership role as a positive stimulus, you can trigger behavior you need for a successful turnaround. As discussed in previous chapters, focusing on a *Quick Wins*, using measurement, observation, and providing feedback to accelerate performance, you will become a positive stimulus.

> **3. QUICK WINS—**
> **Require leaders to implement**
> **systematic feedback**
> **using a tiered approach**

So we recognize the importance of effective feedback for enabling *Quick Wins* and the overall success of a turnaround. In a perfect world, all staff would need the same amount of feedback to achieve the desired state of performance. But in the real world, school leaders should strive to treat their staff *equitably* (as opposed to equally) to reach the desired goals.

Just like it's important to provide differentiated instruction to students to meet their needs, staff require differentiated approaches to feedback to support their needs. In fact, there is an approach called *situational leadership* that nicely supports the need for equitability by recommending a continuum of directive and supportive behavior based on the need of the follower (Hersey, Blanchard, & Johnson, 2001).

But determining the needs of your staff and differentiating your approach can be a challenge, to say the least. For this reason, we recommend using Response to Intervention (RTI) logic as a means of systematically supporting staff based on their need whenever implementing school-wide initiatives.

RTI, a common approach used across many states, is a multi-tiered (Tier I, II, & III) approach that attempts to support academic and behavioral success through universal screening, quick intervention, frequent measurement, and progressively intensive instruction or interventions for students who continue to have difficulty.

This approach can be easily applied during *Quick Wins*:

Tier I provides some universal training (most likely as part of Tier I) to all staff (e.g., teachers), with simple follow-up feedback to shape behavior.

Tier II provides retraining and brief follow-up coaching to a targeted group of educators who are not performing to the established criteria laid out during the initial Tier I training.

Tier III, much like situational leadership, focuses on specific needs of the individual (e.g., managing response rates, using standards and scales, etc.). These staff would receive focused coaching to meet the individual needs of educators who did not respond (perform to standard) to the Tier II intervention.

Let's take a deeper look at the multi-tiered approach, using a familiar concept for getting the most out of your feedback during and following a turnaround.

Tier I—Learning New Skills Requires Practice

Unfortunately, too many teachers and staff are provided "sit and gets" as professional development, and then they are expected to perform a newly learned skill to some established standard. For many years researchers have found there is often far too much theory, and far too little practice during professional development endeavors (Showers, Joyce, & Bennett, 2002). If this worked, we wouldn't be writing this book!

The good news is that, during initial professional development, there are two simple strategies to promote generalization of newly learned and developing skills as part of a Tier I approach. This is important when you are establishing *Quick Wins,* as well as fostering sustainable change.

First: less talk, more practice—During training to build fluency, leaders need to ensure frequent repetition and performance feedback for targeted skills. In other words: less talk, more practice. To engage the teacher in the learning process toward achieving fluency, Parsons, Rollyson, Iverson, and Reid (2013) recommend that skills training occur in this sequence:

1. Require performer to describe the target skill
2. Provide performer with a precise written descriptions of the skill
3. Demonstrate the skill for the performer
4. Require performer to deliberately practice the skill
5. Give performer specific feedback during practice
6. Repeat steps 4 and 5 (practice and feedback) until the skill is mastered

This sequence fosters a *significant gain* of knowledge and skill. When educators understand the expectations and they have the ability to perform the skill, the feedback leaders provide during the normal school day is *much* more likely to significantly improve the effectiveness of the skill. While on the job feedback is often required for generalization of newly learned skills, this training process frequently eliminates the need for more time and resource-consuming strategies used like in-depth coaching and further training.

With a brief shot of **QUICK** feedback from the leadership team that will be discussed shortly, staff will be much more likely to observe meaningful change as a result of their newly acquired skill. Changes like increased student engagement, improved behavior, and gains in academic achievement will strengthen self-efficacy while strengthening the belief in you as a leader.

Second: use walkabouts—The principle behind walkabouts is to increase visibility and provide positive feedback during the initial phases of any new school-wide initiative. What leaders do and say daily as they walk the hallways is far more important than what is said in a meeting. Leaders are constantly evaluated, so this is a time leaders can establish themselves as a positive stimulus by conveying warmth and knowledge in a way that helps staff to feel safe and cared for.

This heightened visibility and use of positive interactions and feedback effectively builds momentum, and any feedback that results in meaningful and positive consequences to staff strengthens belief that the leader is somebody who respects them, is knowledgeable, and can be trusted.

Be aware of your nonverbal behaviors during walkabouts. According to Goman (2011) in the *Silent Language of Leaders*, presidential elections are lost or won not by where the candidate stands on issues, but rather *by the warmth and confidence conveyed during the election.* Behaviorally this means that leaders should use "open body postures, palm-up hand gestures, a full-frontal body orientation, positive eye contact, synchronized movements, head nods, head tilts, and smiles" (Goman, 2011).

By deliberately walking around, leaders are physically present to ask how the staff is doing, how new initiative is going, and focus on *catching staff performing well*. The leadership team can quickly accelerate any new initiative with walkabouts. Since use of feedback as a Tiered strategy supports any new initiative, leaders will find themselves building relationships with their team and supporting them every step of the learning and change process.

This is Tier I—train to fluency to accelerate change. The main point here is any initial training a school leader provides should use these strategies so they can quickly generalize into the classroom.

The QUICK Feedback Approach

To increase the efficiency and effectiveness of feedback while demonstrating you care, use **QUICK** feedback as a Tier I process during walkabouts:

Questions: ask!

Unconditional positive regard: provide it (Rogers, 1956).

Immediate positive reinforcement of any observed improvement in performance: provide it.

Constructive feedback: deliver it to coach staff through minor errors, or when staff solicit it.

Keep feedback brief and meaningful (since a key to this approach is frequency and *brevity.)*

Here's a closer look—

Questions—At the root of questioning during the QUICK feedback process is demonstrating the leader is invested in the well-being of staff as well as the change. Questions can be simple, like *How is your day? How are you doing with the new changes?* or *Do you need help?*

Unconditional Positive Regard—Known as "non-contingent attention" in the behavioral sciences, unconditional positive regard captures the essence of strengthening relationships with team members while establishing the leader as a reinforcer.

Immediate positive reinforcement—Provides high value to those who demonstrate improved performance, and further builds the relationship between the leader and staff.

Constructive Feedback—Gives the leadership the opportunity to correct and then later reinforce performance in a way that helps staff grow. The intent here is to help, not hinder.

Keep feedback brief—Your attention is powerful and in demand. While you want to be available, your time is limited, so by deliberately keeping it brief, you can increase positive interactions with more team members.

Tier II—Feedback Should Be Equitable, Not Equal

Even with excellent training using the approaches above, typically there will be staff who need further support. Such educators who do not respond effectively to your universal Tier I approach, as observed during walkabouts, should then receive additional support as a Tier II QUICK intervention.

Instead of thinning your resources with individual coaching, Tier II efficiently supports educators through a group retrain, followed by frequent but brief follow-up observations with feedback on targeted skills. This group-retrain still uses the skills training listed above, but because many fewer staff are involved, they gain the opportunity to receive increased repetition and feedback to build greater fluency in targeted skills. Moreover, you can focus walkabouts and brief coaching interactions on this group to assist with generalizing their skills into the school or classroom.

Tier III—Performance Management for Ongoing Success

Tier III approaches the managing of staff performance like a coach, using ongoing performance monitoring and feedback. For you, this is not about taking an individual approach to performance, but rather a systematic approach to managing the team's performance. This involves you or designees (e.g. coaches) giving teachers and staff opportunities to demonstrate their skills, provide feedback (in the form of data measurement and graphic feedback as mentioned), and set/reinforce goals to shape targeted skills.

You should see Tier III as your ongoing feedback process, versus the first two tiers, which have an expiration date following training. When instructional coaches are available, you can direct them to staff who need Tier III interventions.

Chapter 7: Quick Wins: Important Strategies and Tactics

Anyone going through a turnaround, regardless of position or tenure at the school, is not easy! Leading a turnaround is equally or more challenging, as the end result depends on your ability to lead. So these final tips are just for you—the one who leads the turnaround, who is faced with daily challenges, who engages educators, staff, and the community to make a positive difference for the future of their school.

Use the 4:1 Rule

During periods of high uncertainty and change, people need more feedback and recognition than usual. They need confirmation that what they are doing is on target and correct. As we mentioned earlier, the 4:1 rule can be very powerful for building change, especially under conditions where morale is low: give positive feedback four times as often as you give constructive feedback.

Target your feedback to a few specific desired behaviors that you would like to see from the person, monitor the behaviors, and if you see improvement, provide that positive feedback. If you like a behavior, but there is still room for improvement, give positive feedback about the improvement: "I've seen progress in the way you've been instructing the new curriculum."

Always keep your feedback positive. Don't say, "I've seen great progress in the way you've been doing X, *but* I think you could be even better." No buts! People will listen for the "but" every time you give positive feedback. (We will come back to the "but" shortly.)

When it comes to constructive feedback, very few of us have ever been formally trained on how to give and receive it. So some of us are unsure of our own skills in this area. Further, during a time of high tension, it's more difficult to provide constructive feedback because people are more likely to react defensively.

But it's important to remember that constructive feedback is necessary for improving results. People will appreciate your constructive feedback if it helps them succeed. Always remember, the intent is to help, not hinder. If you are faced with a defensive person, first recognize that the receiver is probably under stress. That will often lead people to react more defensively than normal. It's important to stay calm and not take his or her reaction personally. Listen to what the person is saying, not only how he's saying it. Respond to the person's concerns in a sensitive way, and be sure to refocus the conversation on the issue at hand when appropriate.

Immediate Feedback Is Best

When delivering feedback, the more immediate the better. When it comes to performance, the best-case scenario is to provide feedback in real time, like a coach would during a game. This lets you reinforce emerging behavior, or the opportunity to alter behavior immediately and then reinforce correct behavior as it occurs later.

While immediacy is important, frequency of feedback is paramount. Providing one opportunity for immediate feedback is not enough to help people learn new skills. Can you imagine a boxing coach showing a fighter how to throw a combination and then expecting them to climb into the ring and effectively perform? Of course not! Learning new skills requires *frequent* and immediate feedback.

While it is unrealistic to think that you can observe all performance immediately, you can create systems using your leadership team and coaches to provide frequent feedback on just a few targeted goals. You can also ask your staff questions about their performance, related to some targeted skill: "How is it working?" "What did you do to make that happen?" "What will you do next time?" (Laipple, 2012). This type of questioning gives you the opportunity to reinforce and possibly give corrective feedback.

Avoid the "Big But" Error

Another very common feedback error is the "big but" error. You've heard it before, and you've probably used it recently. It goes something like: "You did a great job . . . but . . ." Daniels (2000) likens the "but" to a great eraser that effectively eliminates any positive statement that was made beforehand. In fact, using "but" may effectively eliminate the benefits of any positive feedback you give in the future, as the person being praised is simply waiting for the other shoe to drop—the "but." Other "big buts" come in different forms, like "however," "it's just that," "next time," and others. Avoid the "big but" error. Simply eliminate the praise and provide corrective feedback on its own. If you've developed a good relationship using your 4:1 rule, you'll have nothing to worry about!

It's Not What You Say, It's How You Say It!

Using good communication skills to deliver constructive feedback will help you positively influence behavior in any situation. While verbal and written communication skills are important, researchers continue to find that both verbal and nonverbal communication are important to focus on as leaders. How can you improve your communication skills to make your feedback more effective? Here are a couple of tips to guide you.

Keep It Short and Sweet

When you hear a talk or lecture that lasts way too long, you might find yourself quickly losing interest. In fact, you might begin looking for the quickest escape route!

Now, think about the last time you gave someone feedback—how long did you take to deliver the message? Did the person get it? You can immediately increase your effectiveness by utilizing the old saying, *short and sweet. Brief, meaningful* feedback and communications are more effective when influencing behavior, especially when the goal is correction.

Body Language

We talked before about body language, and we'll revisit it here, given the large influence it can have on staff.

During any interaction, especially providing feedback, body language becomes *incredibly* important. Our bodies are much like a transmitter that is constantly pumping out signals. You must be aware of these signals that you are transmitting, and understand their impact on the people around you.

My (this is Paul speaking) young son once asked me, "Daddy, why do you look angry?" At that moment, I looked into the nearest mirror and realized my son was right—I *did* look angry! The problem was, I wasn't angry at all. In fact, I was just in deep thought. I will never know how many times people thought I was mad, when in actuality I was just thinking. Be aware of how your facial expression looks to others.

Behaviors like crossing your arms and knitting your brows are commonly perceived as coercive, and can quickly put your staff and students on the defensive.

When giving constructive feedback, try relaxing your body language and addressing your staff or students calmly. Some students (and adults, imagine that!) may actually want to get you upset. You may have witnessed this occur when some young couples argue, or if you've ever worked with students labeled "defiant."

When these students and adults recognize even the tiniest behavioral cues that indicate you may be getting upset, you can be sure that they will quickly "push those buttons" to evoke your reaction in the same way buttons are pushed on game controllers. Each time your body language changes, even slightly, you are communicating. For whatever reason, there are some individuals who may actually find an angry or irritated response gratifying. The key here is not to react, but remain calm.

Chapter 8: Quick Wins in Action: Improving School Climate and Culture

At the beginning of this book we introduced the *Quick Wins* Matrix Tool to assist you with identifying and evaluating potential *Quick Wins*. Specifically, we suggested that you identify *Quick Wins* based on:

- The Impact the *Quick Win* will bring to the school
- The Visibility the *Quick Win* has to all who are watching the school's turnaround
- The Effort to implement the *Quick Win* is easily achievable using the schools and districts resources.

This section of the book is dedicated to providing stories and examples of *Quick Wins* we have effectively applied. The goal here is to bring the principles of *Quick Wins* to life through detailed and sometimes humorous real-life examples and experiences.

Hallway Duty

One *Quick Win* that has consistently met these criteria in schools we have supported is *duty in common areas.* If through your **QuickWOC** you identified *hallway transitions,* here is how you can implement this *Quick Win* at your school.

Hallway duty is a pain for many, but it is critical to a school turnaround. Hallway duty has been proven to positively impact student achievement, while simultaneously making school staff's job easier. We have observed that transitions (particularly arrival) often directly correlate with student achievement. Not only can hallway duty provide a measure of culture and climate; a quick observation can reveal who has consistently enforced rules and reinforced appropriate behavior.

Hallway duty is an opportunity to watch student behavior around particular staff members. Are students tucking their shirts in, walking (not running) when they see that staff member, or going out of their way to say hello? Why is this important? Student arrival and transitioning at school is critical for establishing desired behavior throughout the school day. When staff fails to consistently reinforce the right behavior, the wrong things can occur, snowballing and generalizing into the classroom at a very deep level.

We can't tell you how many times we have heard students, after being redirected for misbehavior, complain, "Well Mr. Lassitude always lets us . . . ." It's probably not that Mr. Lassitude "lets them," but more likely the illusion of permission—from failure to establish expectations, or failure to apply consistent reinforcement and correction of behavior. (Remember: doing *nothing* is doing *something*.)

When staff fails to reinforce and correct behavior, noncompliance will spread like wildfire as other students perceive they don't have to follow the rules either. This can have immediate effect and lasting, erosive impact on staff morale, school climate, and student achievement. This is a classic lack of leadership.

When transitioning procedures (like school arrival) are implemented correctly, the presence of staff can serve as a cue telling the students how they should behave in the same way a traffic light tells drivers how to behave (e.g., a red traffic light tells drivers to stop).

In the field of Organizational Behavior Management (OBM), the presence of someone who holds a specific role in the eyes of others (teacher to student, supervisor to employee), can have a serious impact on behavior—good, bad, and in some cases ugly. Imagine being at your duty post without having to redirect misbehavior. Your role becomes more of a positive start to the student's day, saying hi, good morning, and asking how they are doing.

It sounds like a fantasy for some, but after seeing this occur in many school turnarounds, it becomes a real outcome when leaders deploy such *Quick Wins,* effectively shaping desired behaviors and making their jobs easier! Implemented appropriately, *Quick Wins* can improve arrival and transitioning procedures, resulting in:

- Stronger relationships between staff and students
- Improved academic achievement (students comes to class ready to learn)
- Improved school climate (teachers and students share a common positive perspective on the school, based on safe and positive interactions within common areas)
- Stronger self-efficacy among staff regarding behavior management
- Staff become a positive stimulus

Conquering the Cafeteria

If you have worked at a school where misbehavior is common, there is a good chance that you dread visiting the cafeteria during student lunch, or frequently experience dismay at the Pandora's box of behavior resulting from poorly managed cafeterias during the latter part of the school day. Make no mistake, overstimulation in the cafeteria has the potential to negatively affect every student and staff. This inevitably will impact student achievement.

Student lunch is a good place where an observer might take the "temperature" of the school. Negative climate (shared perceptions) and culture (shared behaviors) have the potential to slowly creep down hallways, into the front office, and eventually into the classroom.

If that sounds like an ad for a horror flick, then we have the same vision. If it elicited a visceral internal response, you might be suffering from PTSD, likely as a result of the never-ending uphill battle that some might call Hamburger Hill (since we are talking about lunch!).

The UN-Silent Lunch

In fact, while observing the cafeteria under less-structured conditions, one might observe some well-meaning staff march to the front of the cafeteria, pick up the microphone as if it were a weapon, and then forcibly declare "that's it, SILENT LUNCH!" Every time we see this we feel like yelling out, "please put the microphone down and step away . . . slowly." We've seen this played out many times across many schools, especially elementary schools. The funny thing is: it never works!

We are not sure what happens to folks when they enter the cafeteria. Most of them are great people who typically behave benevolently, at least outside of the cafeteria! However, once they cross the threshold that separates the cafeteria from the real world, it's like they enter a parallel dimension . . . one where an alternative self takes over, one who prefers reprimand to reinforcement. Think of it *Invasion of the Body Snatchers,* or a never-ending episode of *Breaking Bad!*

In one cafeteria, we experienced a bit of a *Twilight Zone* after observing countless reprimands of students by staff. Then we saw a fair damsel who we caught smiling and praising a couple of students. We were busy with a student, so we asked a colleague to let her know that we recognized and appreciated her positive interactions with the students. To our chagrin, she actually began to cry! Can you believe that? Cry!!! Talk about a parallel universe.

But think about this. If you are part of a cafeteria culture that has slowly drifted to the dark side, your efforts at positive interaction with students might be perceived as weakness, or even anti-administration. That is exactly what she later expressed to us. She also mentioned it was "so nice to hear positive feedback." Apparently she (like the students) was positive feedback–deprived . . . further evidence of a negative culture.

After witnessing similar scenes played out across other schools, we decided we needed to intervene. Like any good behaviorists, we began collecting data on variables related to student and staff behavior. Since the "silent lunch" demands were ineffective (actually doing more harm than good), and appeared to be random, we decided it might be helpful to collect data on the decibel levels in the cafeteria that evoked the "silent lunch" command from staff.

What did we find? No evident pattern regarding the decibel level that prompted staff to initiate the punishment. Decibel levels were all over the place, and based on cultural norms, mood, perception, and noise tolerance of the attending staff.

So we collected data on the time—specifically, how long it took for students to begin talking again after the staff declared "silent lunch." Any guesses? Almost reliably, about 45–60 seconds later, a few students would begin whispering, and then a few more, and pretty soon the whole cafeteria was chatting away. The result… just hit replay. The same staff said the same thing and got the same results. We think we are into *Groundhog Day* territory now. Fortunately, we were armed with the science of behavior to break the cycle.

The staff were getting caught up in what classroom management guru Glenn Latham (1998) called the Criticism Trap, whereby the tendency is to "catch students behaving bad" as opposed to recognizing their "good" or improved behavior. Perhaps they had not been trained and coached to fluency in basic procedures for managing behavior. There might be rules on the wall, and possibly "training" generally related to behavior, but there is no way they would continue to use ineffective strategies like "silent lunch" if they knew better.

Nobody wants to waste time consistently managing chronic misbehavior. We believe that administrators, teachers, and support staff truly desire to perform well, for students to achieve, and for misbehavior to remain at a minimum. School employees at all levels just need to be taught (not told) better. So the sections below provide a plan . . .

The Secret Sauce: Teamwork

As leaders, behavior analysts, and coaches who have been successful in turning around failing schools, we can tell you that improving the behavior in any common area within the school requires teamwork. "There is no 'I' in team" fits the cafeteria, as no one person can fix it.

Many times we've walked into a cafeteria and an administrator or staff member has said, "Thank goodness you are here! Can you get these kids to behave?" The answer is no, we can't! ... at least not sustainably.

Much like the staff member who grabs the mic and demands a silent lunch, anything we do solo will only result in a temporary fix. We love coach John Wooden's story on the importance of teamwork where he notes that, despite being stacked with superstars like Kobe Bryant, Karl Malone, and Shaq, the 2004 USA Olympic Basketball team failed to win a gold medal. The reason, as Wooden notes: USA sent great players, while the countries who won the gold and silver medals sent great teams. Unless you have a very small cafeteria, managing cafeteria behavior in schools that struggle with misbehavior is simply too much for one person, even a superstar. While the person who continually grabs the mic to demand silent lunch may be practicing fruitless behavior, it's been our experience that they are often doing their best to carry the ball by themselves, despite being surrounded by a team.

In their mind they are taking action while the rest of the cafeteria team sits on their hands. It's not that the rest of the team is lazy or weak. More likely, they do not possess the self-efficacy for managing student behavior, as a result of limited mastery experiences. In other words, if they have not seen their efforts work in the past, they likely do not believe in their ability to manage behavior.

And let's not forget the arm-chair quarterbacking that occurs from some administrators or staff who are regularly in the cafeteria. It's easy to say "do this, do that". But managing the cafeteria requires more than talk. It demands a systematic and consistent approach from those on the front line, from the teacher who leads students to the cafeteria, and from administrators who structure and support all efforts.

Strategic Action Planning with the End in Mind

We've heard this called different things by behaviorists— reverse behavior engineering, results-behavior map, alignment matrix, backwards planning—but *planning with the end in mind* is becoming common in education as teachers plan their lessons with student learning in mind. This process helps those tasked with developing a cafeteria routine or fixing a current structure to align the actions of everyone who directly or indirectly impacts student behavior in the cafeteria.

We've seen great school improvement plans that garnered poor results because the plans were never followed. Educators and staff need to believe the plan is workable and that they can implement it. This strengthens self-efficacy as well as belief in the plan. Fundamental to the development of self-efficacy and collective efficacy (Bandura, 1997) are performance-based training, coaching, strategic use measurement, and reinforcement. To observe the plan working, *strategic action planning with the end in mind* requires determining which results are to be impacted, the student and staff behaviors that will move these measures, and how feedback will be provided to reinforce or adjust the plan. We will cover this process in the following sections.

The Value of Leading Indicators

When you create a cafeteria management plan, determine your measures. Then divide them into leading indicators and lagging indicators:

> ***Leading indicators:*** think about *what you are seeing now* to let you know you are on the right track
>
> ***Lagging indicators:*** think about *what future results will be impacted* by the leading indicators

Leading indicators are related to student behavior and staff performance. These might be measures like number of students in their seats, number of students put on time-out, number of staff at their posts, or frequency of adult-to-student interaction (remember, the recommended ratio of positive to negative interactions is 4:1).

Collecting this data can be simple. You might divide the cafeteria into a grid and observe different areas for 10 minutes, while using pencil-and-paper to record incidents of student behavior and frequency of staff behavior. Repeat this process during different lunch times.

Lagging indicators are outcomes that these leading indicators will impact. Lagging data includes measures like discipline referrals and social validity measures (i.e., staff perceptions).

At this point you might be thinking, "They're talking data again. We don't have time for that. We need action *right now!*" Although it is a four-letter word, data is your friend—you can use it to help your cafeteria improve. The fact is, you don't have time to *not* collect data. Like a soccer scoreboard, this data allows you to *see* your progress, or lack thereof. Good data lets you observe even the smallest changes.

When things are going well, students and staff can be reinforced for even the smallest changes (this is called "shaping" in the behavioral sciences). If things aren't going well, use the data to adjust your game plays. If are considering using this Quick Win and you are approaching a natural break (e.g., winter break), you can collect data now (about 3 days' worth should be adequate) and implement your strategic plan immediately following the break. The "now" data can be used as a baseline later.

Once you've nailed down the leading indicators, as yourself, "what must the cafeteria staff do to improve student behavior?" We can help you here…

Staff Performance in the Cafeteria

Here are some basics:

Staff should know precisely what to do, how to do it, where to stand and walk, what they should monitor, and exactly what they should say and do under specific conditions (more on this later).

Establish staff expectations regarding what they should do when students are behaving well, and how to correct misbehavior when it occurs.

The main thing is consistency. If staff fail to reinforce desirable behavior, you are unlikely to see improvement in behavior. If staff fail to effectively correct misbehavior, you will almost definitely see more problem behaviors because the perception will be that the misbehavior is being condoned.

The positive impact of staff performance must be visible to them. If not, there is a good chance staff will stop performing, or perform only when you are present and watching.

Thus, we make the following recommendations:

When students are behaving well (following rules and expectations), staff should:

- *Provide non-contingent attention to strengthen desirable behavior.* For example, sincerely asking students about their weekend, how school is going, or if they watched the latest game. Though this is termed "non-contingent" attention, it is actually contingent on rule-following behavior. In other words, don't strike up a conversation when a student is out of his assigned area or yelling out across the cafeteria. This might inadvertently shape up more misbehavior! The point of noncontingent attention is that it provides students positive attention for desirable behaviors.

- ***Specifically praise the behavior that you want to see.*** While some folks use the microphone only for correcting misbehavior, we recommend the opposite. Try to use the mic to reinforce improvements in behavior. The same person who picks up the mic 5 minutes into lunch after students begin screaming across to other tables might use it 4 minutes into lunch to recognize and thank students for being "responsible" by speaking with only the students at their table. The time interval here can be progressively increased. (By the way, don't waste your breath if the praise isn't sincere. Nobody wants praise if they don't believe the person delivering it actually means it. To us it is worse than being reprimanded!)

When students are misbehaving, it is staffs' job to correct misbehavior:

- ***Consistently***—this means *do not ignore* misbehavior. We hear seasoned educators recommend "ignoring" all the time as a behavioral intervention. We want to be a little more precise in its use. From our perspective, "planned ignoring" is great when students who desire your attention are misbehaving for the purpose of obtaining your attention. But ignoring students who are misbehaving and do not desire your attention is an instant fail. If staff do not consistently correct misbehavior, it spreads like wildfire. It also subverts staff who are consistently attempting to correct misbehavior. The sure sign of this is when little Nicole says, "well, Ms. Schrugg lets me do it," that is a leading indicator that something needs to be corrected.

- *Respectfully*—always treat students with dignity and respect, of course—but this does not mean you should not correct misbehavior. It means avoiding tones that are sarcastic and condescending, and correcting misbehavior in a businesslike manner. It also means sticking to the 4:1 rule. If you correct misbehavior, make it a point to get back to that student in the future with 4 more positive interactions as illustrated above. Remember, you are trying to create a cafeteria culture where everyone wants to be.

Teacher Behavior

Are you thinking, "but teachers aren't in the cafeteria, so why is this part of their responsibility?" If you suspect teachers feel this way, you may want to explain to them how common areas will have a major impact throughout the school, that pushes into their classroom like a running back driving for a first down. Help them understand that being a team player in this area will have a positive impact in their class and across the school campus. Also, tell them not to worry…their part is relatively easy:

> ***Teachers should teach cafeteria rules and expectations for the first days of school.*** Use a map of the cafeteria to explain transition routines and behavioral expectations.
> ***Teachers should remind students of these expectations just prior to the students transitioning into the cafeteria.*** In a relay race, it is the responsibility of the baton holder to transition the baton smoothly to the next runner to maintain continuity and velocity in a race.

Reclaiming the Cafeteria: The Plan

The final part of your plan is where we believe most schools fail. This is the actual development of a plan with these elements, training staff to fluency in reinforcing and correcting behavior, and observing and helping these folks perform to their best ability.

Remember, staff in the cafeteria must know precisely what to do, believe they can do it, and believe they can positively impact the cafeteria behavior. It's not enough to tell them what they should do, and hope they will do it.

Folks involved in this part of the plan should see themselves as coaches, preparing to bring out the best in their team.

We began ***Quick Wins*: Conquering the Cafeteria** with a rant on the overuse of punishment in the *Silent Lunch Fallacy*. Then we started laying out plan for Reclaiming the Cafeteria. Now we'll lay out key elements to include in the final part of your plan.

Many of the processes covered here are areas where we strongly believe most schools fail. This has to do with the actual development of the plan (e.g., a plan with these elements), training staff to fluency in regards to reinforcing and correcting behavior, and observing and helping these folks perform to their best ability. Remember, staff in the cafeteria must know precisely what to do, believe they can do it, and believe they can positively impact the cafeteria behavior. Folks involved in this part of the plan should think about themselves as coaches who are seeking to bring out the best in their team.

Develop a map—To make things easy, include a cafeteria map and simple plan that include the following:

> ***Traffic flow***—Attempt to have students enter in one direction and leave in another. Keeping traffic moving in a single direction is a simple fix for many problems. Simply add arrows indicating student movement patterns.
>
> ***Staff posts***—Write the staff's name in the desired location. If you know there are "hot" areas, try placing your most skilled staff in those areas. As other staff become more skilled, you can rotate these areas weekly, monthly, or quarterly to avoid burnout.
>
> ***Areas staff should monitor***—While staff are collectively responsible for supporting appropriate

behavior across the cafeteria, having an assigned area to monitor allows for more focused observations.

Expectations regarding staff behavior—Specifically, where they should walk as they monitor, and what they should say and do as outlined earlier.

Behavior staff will focus on to reinforce—We wrote earlier about how staff can reinforce through non-contingent attention and specific praise. Try to match your praise with what is desirable to the students. We divide praise into 4 types:

> ***Quiet praise***—good for older students or those who do not like to be praised in public. A subtle thumbs up, well-timed nod of the head, or simple smile following a desirable behavior are examples.
>
> ***Individual praise***—simply providing praise to an individual who is displaying a desirable behavior (remember to be behavior-specific). Be careful not to fall into the trap of correcting a misbehavior, and then only praising the appropriate behavior once the student displays it. If you need to praise a student for following the directive (following redirection may be a "new" behavior for some students) try to differentiate this praise from the praise you typically provide. For example, make it less enthusiastic, or minimize your eye contact.

Group praise—just like it sounds, you might praise a group of students for doing well or having shown improvement: "the students at table 2 are on-point today with their conversation levels!"

Pivot praise—praising a student who is behaving as expected, as prompt to a nearby student who is not. When the student begins following the expectation, the staff then "pivots" to that student and praises. This tactic, like the planned ignoring strategy discussed earlier, is typically best for students who desire your attention. It is intended to avoid giving an off-task or misbehaving student desirable attention for undesirable behavior.

Rules and expectations regarding student behavior—The behaviors that give you the most cluck for your buck are those that are incompatible with the most common misbehaviors: communicating loudly and leaving an assigned area. To avoid these misbehaviors, focus staff on reinforcing, using the strategies above, as they encourage students naturally to remain in their area and communicate at a reasonable voice level. Consider embedding the following in your rules and expectations:

Students face forward with their feet on the ground
Students request permission to leave their seat
Students speak only to peers directly next to or in front

Develop a menu of corrective consequences—develop a simple menu of consequences that are aligned with the magnitude of misbehaviors common to the cafeteria. For example, a consequence for running in the cafeteria might be to walk back; a consequence for yelling across tables might be a brief time out. Remember, avoid "silent lunch" as the go-to behavior management tool.

If you must incorporate silent lunch as part of your plan, make sure it is not a marathon. Brief is best, like most time-outs (that's essentially what a silent lunch is—time out away from social reinforcement). Try 1–2 minutes, with the expectation that all students follow that expectation. If a student from the group talks, simply remind all students of the expectation and reset the time for 1 minute. Time-outs can also be applied at the smaller group and individual level (a table or a student that has been reminded and then warned about an expectation). Again, brevity is best. Time-outs that are too long result in students learning they do not need to follow the expectation, as staff typically do not have the resources to ensure students maintain the time-out as expected for the designated time.

For individual time-outs, 3-5 minutes works well. If you find there are only a few students from the group not following expectations of a whole group time-out, individualize their time-outs and avoid punishing the entire group.

Getting staff to believe they can do it—Albert Bandura's research (1986) demonstrated that self-efficacy—or belief in one's ability to accomplish a task—is one of the biggest success predictors. But how do you develop self-efficacy?

The answer is simple, and it doesn't require hypnosis or special psychological strategies. It requires deliberately structuring conditions that allow for staff to receive training in the concept and purpose of the plan, and then providing ample opportunity for staff to practice (with feedback) the skills required to implement the plan.

I recommend practicing in the cafeteria. Require staff to stand, walk, and monitor the area designated in the plan. Create real-life scenarios (I'm sure you have plenty) and practice staff responses. These scenarios should include staff responses that reinforce desired student behavior and strengthen relationships, as well as those intended to correct misbehavior.

The goal is to provide as many scenarios and practice opportunities as are needed to get staff to respond without correction from the coach. Once staff can apply these strategies quickly and independent of feedback, they should have enough tools to get them through the initial days back from break—a small window when student misbehavior is typically at a low.

Getting staff to believe they can positively impact behavior—
While it is important for staff to have the requisite knowledge and skills to change cafeteria behavior, they must also believe that they can actually do it on game day.

Suppose we spend months demonstrating to staff effective techniques for flying. We practice flapping our arms and getting a running start. Staff become very proficient in the flying procedures and flawlessly demonstrate them under practice conditions. But on the big day, we are lined up atop the cliff ready for launch . . . and there is a 100% chance that no one will jump. The reason is obvious: they do not truly believe they can fly!

Our point is, if staff is going to implement procedures after training, without our prodding them, they must believe that they can do it, and that a positive outcome will result. This is at the root of what we call "grit." You won't see grit if folks do not believe their efforts will bear fruit. However, if they believe they can do it and value the outcome, they will push through adversity to reach the goal.

As part of your cafeteria plan, leaders must help launch and secure designees to support and coach the initial implementation. Having a vision, a plan, and training is a great start, but it is insufficient for success. While staff may be been trained to some level of fluency, they will tend to fall back on their old habits. Administrators and designees should act like coaches, helping their team perform well enough to be successful.

While these "coaches" can model once or twice how to perform a specific skill under actual live cafeteria conditions, they need to refrain from correcting student misbehavior themselves. At this point, staff should know what to do. This is important for building self-efficacy and helping the staff develop instructional control.

It is important that students view all adults in the cafeteria as having authority, not just administrators and others tasked with "coaching" the cafeteria. Instructional control will naturally develop through consistency of reinforcement and correction applied by each staff.

For example, rather than asking a student to sit facing forward, the coach should point out the student to cafeteria staff and ask them to correct the behavior. If the monitor has already asked the student to sit facing forward and the student is again turned around yelling to another table, a good coach would ask the monitor what their next response should be. If they provide an incorrect response, the coach might use Socratic questioning to enhance critical thinking skills, or simply say "since you've already redirected the student, you should now provide a warning" and then ask the monitor to quickly state what the warning would be. For example, "Billy, I've asked you once to sit facing forward and speak to the students at your table. If you do, you can remain seated here. If you don't, I will have to require you to sit in the time-out section against the wall for 5 minutes." These responses should be pre-planned and part of your cafeteria plan.

Once the cafeteria folks are performing adequately, it is up to the coach to help them see the positive impact of their collective efforts. It is at this point that the measures we discussed earlier will become your best friend, like a coach referring to the scoreboard who says "look team, the plays you are running are working. We are winning!"

By pumping back measures that demonstrate improved behavior, staff will begin believing in themselves and their collective effort. Sometimes improvement is hard to see, because staff suffering from bias confirmation (the tendency to confirm their existing beliefs) may focus only on the negative, like "we knew these kids wouldn't behave." They may still see a few students yelling across tables and believe that things are the same as ever. But data indicating a 50% reduction of out-of-seat behavior, for example, is almost certain to have a positive influence and strengthen belief in the system as well as the collective efficacy of the team.

Leading indicators to reinforce staff performance are most effective when used immediately in the beginning, then be faded to daily and weekly. Use lagging indicators monthly as an ongoing measure of results. A short email to the team and the school from the principal might say something like, "as a result of the collective efforts of the cafeteria staff, teachers, and coaches, we've had a 37% reduction in cafeteria and afternoon referrals! Well done!!" Using these strategies will also strengthen belief in the administrator or designee who has led the cafeteria change effort.

* * *

We hope you have found this chapter on cafeteria behavior helpful. If you are disappointed that we did not focus more on "noise level" in the cafeteria, it is because we personally believe that students should be able to talk, and not in a "whisper-like" voice. Cafeteria is a time for socialization. We believe lunchtime is recharge time for students, not for staff.

However, if you feel that noise level is a problem in your cafeteria, here is what we recommend: Purchase a decibel reader. There are a variety out there. One that I found very useful was attached to a traffic light. It remained green until the noise level moved beyond a preset point. When this happened, the light would emit a sound and turn yellow. If the noise level did not return to the predetermined level within a few seconds, the light would move to red.

In one school we supported, when the light went red, students were required to remain silent for one minute, or until the light returned to green. And when the light remained on green for 15 minute intervals, the grade groups in the cafeteria would receive "stars" that would eventually allow them access to group reinforcers like music played in the cafeteria, temporarily changing seats, or even an ice cream day.

Without some measure with feedback, it is improbable that students will be able "check" their voice levels; moreover, staff are more likely to correct noise levels based on their mood or perception, which is often inaccurate.

Like anything else, this is just a tool. Without the processes indicated in this article, we don't know of any tool that will consistently work. Case in point: we observed the same stop light used at another school. In that school, the students would actually take great joy in speaking louder in attempts to get the light to change colors. The staff response to this was to readjust the decibel meter so the students could not trigger it, even if they were yelling—a nice example of students shaping staffs' behavior!

Starting with the Leader in the Mirror

Hopefully we've hammered this point home: school leaders are *critical* to staff performance and the resulting student achievement. Some research has even found that a school leader can be responsible for up to 25% of student achievement. One person!

Unfortunately, the field of education is having a very hard time keeping school leaders around. According to the *Hechinger Report,* nearly *30%* of principals leading "troubled" schools leave every year, and *half of all principals* leave their job inside of five years. Being a school leader is a tough job, especially in high-poverty or failing schools. Compensation is clearly not enough to help many be successful and stay.

Make no mistake, school leaders *want* to be successful. If you are reading this book, it is a sure indicator that *you* want to be successful. School leaders understand very well the ramifications of success, or lack thereof, to themselves, staff, families, students, and the community.

Telling school leaders to be better or pointing the finger at them only increases their attrition rate. Unfortunately, this is an approach employed by district leaders who do not understand the fundamental principles of human behavior. Districts would be best served by focusing greater energy toward developing and coaching school leaders to bring out their best so they can bring out the best in others. They need help!

Though research on school leadership has underscored the importance of leadership preparation and development for school district leaders (Rebore, 2012), many leadership development and personal growth programs exist as a compliance measure rather than as a powerful process with the potential to benefit every student and staff within a district. This is especially unfortunate, since many school leaders are reporting their college and pre-service programs did not prepare them for the demands of the position (Grisson & Harrington, 2010).

Leadership programs likely will need to rethink their preparation curriculum. Until that time, it is clear that many school leaders need to be given greater support, or take the bull by the horns themselves to deepen their skillset. Since school districts are often stretched thin, employing simple, it is wise to employ efficient strategies that can have a large impact on performance and the resulting student achievement.

The Disconnect Without Measurement

Unfortunately, there appears to be disconnects between many leaders' self-perception and the perception of their followers. Having an objective perception of oneself is obviously a challenging endeavor. Some leaders may see themselves as eagles soaring high, with a bird's-eye view on progress toward the vision, mission, and goals of a school. However, staff may have a different vision. From their perspective, if the leader walks like a duck . . . and talks like a duck . . . then the leader must be a duck!

In other words, your image reflected in the mirror may not be what your staff sees. This may only be their perception, not rooted in reality. But like the old cliché goes, perception is reality. It is more common than you might think for a school leader's intention to be mismatched with how teachers and staff actually view them and receive their messages.

Unfortunately, people do not judge school leaders by their intentions, but by their impact. For this reason, you *must* have a way to measure your impact upon others beyond end-of-year student achievement scores. If schools and districts measure your impact only on results, they may miss your full impact . . . at the expense of students, staff, and greater leadership development. If you are a school leader, you *must* receive feedback on your leadership performance so you know what you are doing well, and where you can focus growth. And if you discover staffs' perceptions are not aligned with reality, you can use this data to quickly exercise damage control to reshape perceptions through some well-timed and effective communication. This is a *Quick Win!*

Developing Leaders through Measurement

Whatever approach a school district decides to use for leadership development (and we hope it employs real behavioral science!), they *must* have a system for measuring leadership effectiveness as a tool for providing feedback and coaching to school leaders. Since there is a good chance they don't, the 360-degree feedback process (commonly used in the business world) is a simple, cost-effective instrument you can use to examine and grow, using data based on the perceptions of your followers and others.

Also called multisource or multi-rater feedback, a 360-degree instrument can gather feedback from a variety of people who commonly interact with you and other leaders. This might include a variety of staff like superintendents, assistant superintendents, directors, coordinators, teachers, paraprofessionals, and maintenance, as well as parents and students.

Analysis of the feedback can be used as a formative assessment to guide your own leadership development. For any district leaders who may be reading this, it is important to remember this type of measurement and feedback should be strategically employed to help school leaders grow, not used as a hammer or other tool to demonstrate to the leader that they are not measuring up (Alimo-Metcalfe, 1998; Edwards, 1996).

Thus, it is critical for senior district leadership to stress to all involved in the supervision and coaching of school leaders that the 360 feedback tool is not an evaluation tool for hiring or firing principals, but rather a powerful opportunity for leadership development (Moore, 2009). In fact, those tasked with coaching leadership should also be provided some sort of measurement and feedback related to the effectiveness of their coaching!

Essential Questions to Include in Every School Leader's 360 Feedback

There are a variety of 360 feedback tools on the market. Whichever you might choose, we recommend including the following questions as part of any measurement tool for assessing and helping leaders grow:

1. My school leader provides clear expectations of my role and responsibilities toward the success of the school.
2. My school leader supports me by providing the resources I need to make things happen.
3. My school leader enables my professional growth through professional development opportunity, coaching, and mentoring.
4. My school leader monitors performance and gives me ongoing performance-based feedback, both positive and constructive.

5. My school leader communicates to me and my peers consistently about the overall performance of the school.
6. My school leader takes time to directly observe me in action, not to scrutinize but to optimize my performance.
7. My school leader provides ample reinforcement in the form of recognition, positive feedback, and support when I need help.

Remember, the measure of a leader is ultimately found in the performance of his or her followers (Daniels & Daniels, 2007). So it is important for school leaders to receive feedback on their leadership behaviors so they can adjust or improve to bring out the best in those around them.

For leaders to assess and improve their own professional growth, use of 360 degree feedback tools can provide simple yet powerful leading indicators of their leadership. Using this data to improve leadership behaviors can be a *Quick Win* for improving staff performance, student achievement, and leadership effectiveness. With these tools in hand, you can measure and guide continued personal and organizational growth, **starting with the leader in the mirror.**

Customer Service and Curb Side Appeal

It is common knowledge that the first interactions people have when they enter your school is with the staff in the front office. This position can be very powerful as it frequently represents the "face" of the school. Positive interactions in the front office serve to strengthen relationships with the community. One positive interaction can literally connect a missing link; however, one negative interaction can break the chain. As such, it is important to remember it's not only "whacha say," but "howya say it." Specifically, your kinesics (body language) and tone, volume, and cadence are at the heart of communication.

Welcoming Parents, Students, and Community Members

When anyone comes to your school, it is important they feel welcome. The climate of the front office should feel "warm" and inviting. The following are essential for creating this type of climate in any school:

> *Smiling at parents, students and visitors when they enter the front office*
> *Greeting them. For example, "Good morning," "good afternoon," "we'll be right with you."*
> *Offering assistance. For example, "What can I do for you," "how can I help you Mom."*

When the Phone Rings

Much like the front desk folks are the "face" of a school, they are often the "voice" as well! When people call, it is important they are treated with respect and kindness, a kind of "at your service" attitude. When your staff answer the phone, be sure they convey that attitude and use greetings like:

> *"Good Morning! Central Neighborhood School, how may I assist you"*
> *"It is a wonderful day at Central Neighborhood School! How may I assist you."*

Listen to Parents when they are Upset

Effective customer service starts by listening to what parents have to say about their needs, wants or concerns. If you can provide complete and honest answers to their questions, you strengthen trust and further establish your school's standing with them. Often times the honest answer might be "I'm not sure." This is OK. Nobody has all of the answers!! Being open and honest increases the likelihood the parents will want to listen to school representatives in the future. In addition, parents are almost never upset with your front desk folks, so help them to avoid taking it personal! This can be difficult, but it's achievable and worth the effort. When it comes to issues related to people's children, emotions can mount. Often times the issue can be directly related to miscommunication between the home and the school. School personnel should be a model for all. When parents are upset, front office folks may try doing or saying the following:

> *As the parent's volume goes up, they bring their volume down*
> *Use of facial expressions and voice tones that express concern.*

Saying things like:

> *"Mom, you look upset. Let me find somebody who can help you with this."*
> *"Is there anything I can do to help you?"*
> *"While I don't have the answer, I can contact _____ to find out."*
> *"Dad, please know I am doing my very best to help you."*

If parents are using inappropriate language or are highly escalated, they might be told:

> *"Let me see if I can get one of our administrators to help you immediately."*

All school personnel (administrators too!) should avoid saying things like:

> *"Calm down."*

> *"If you would just give me a minute."*

This kind of response is likely to have the opposite of the intended effect as parents will usually escalate if they are told this….and we don't blame them!

Be Flexible

All districts and schools have policies and procedures in place that govern the day to day routines. These are meant to create order and safety at the school site. However, there are times when judgment must be used. Flexibility (as opposed to hyper-rigid adherence to policy and procedure) strengthens relationships and fosters loyalty. If your front office personnel are unsure, tell them they should seek out an administrator. Here are examples of exceptional and reasonable cases where flexibility might be justified:

School begins at 8:45. A parent drops a student off at 8:46 and does not come into the school to sign the student in because the parent is injured

A parent has an emergency and must check the child out at 2:50, prior to the 3:10 pick-up policy

Provide Quick Responses

When front office personnel are unable to provide a quick response to a parent, they may become frustrated…even though the front office staff are typically not to blame! Schools are large and complex systems and sometimes "things" just take time to happen. As a parent, this can be frustrating. Think about it. Have you ever been on hold or waiting for a business to return your call only to become agitated from lack of a timely response? This can give the impression that the business does not value you. Parents are likely to feel the same way. When front office personnel are unable to provide a quick response, they should keep the parent informed and use an empathy statement. They might try saying something like:

"I'm sorry it's taking so long. I know it must be frustrating. Please know we are working on it."

"I would be concerned as well. Let me see how I can help."

Be Humble and Apologize when Mistakes Happen
Look, it might not have been the front office personnel's fault (or yours either). But does that matter? If the parent has suffered or is unhappy because of something that happened at your school, that's a reason to apologize—in a meaningful way. Any school personnel (this includes you!) should tell them in all sincerity—as a representative of the school—that they are sorry and they'll do their best to make sure it doesn't happen again. That's a powerful symbolic gesture that you and your personnel have the highest standards and consider yourselves accountable for service and support.

Frequently Asked Questions and Responses
Finally, at your school it might be a good idea to create a FAQ's sheet that can be posted in the front office or distributed to parents as needed. This sheet might have common questions like the following with responses that fit the context of your school:

1. Can I walk my child to class?
2. Can I get work for my child?
3. Can I observe my child in class?
4. Can I see the principal now?
5. Can I pick up my student before dismissal?
6. Why do I always have to provide my ID?
7. Can I change my child's transportation?
8. How do I get my child tested?
9. Can I speak to the teacher now?
10. Can you give my child medication?

Front office personnel are an extremely valuable part of your school. They can often foster a strong connection between the home and the school. Though it's often said "don't judge a book by its cover," human nature tends to do exactly that. Invest in your front office folks as they are the "cover" of your school. Train them. Help them by posting visual aids around the front office as reminders (e.g. smiley faces or greeting reminders by the phone). And when you see them effectively applying these strategies, recognize them. Provide them reinforcing feedback. Treat them as if they are your customer. It's been our experience that the most effective leaders share a concern and seek to bring out the best in all stakeholders. Helping to bring out the best in your front desk staff can be an immediate *Quick Win!*

Final Thoughts

We believe that good leaders help people, great leaders help people help themselves, and the best leaders help create more leaders. By taking a *Quick Wins* approach and developing leadership and staff skills as described in this book, success is a matter of "when," not "if."

If you've read this book and are thinking, "well, great, but what about sustainability?" We have good news for you. You have just read the formula. Initially you identified the "low-hanging fruit" of your school to gain momentum, build trust, and strengthen belief. To create sustainability, use the *Quick Wins Matrix* to determine where you might gain your next-largest return on investment. All other processes remain the same. Simply repeat them!

Needless to say, we never claim that turnaround is easy. However, taking a science-based, systematic approach to turnaround results in better performance, better staff satisfaction, and long-term results. We are big believers that *Quick Wins* is about the people who make it all happen, and for the people who we serve as educators and leaders of our community.

Thanks for reading. We wish you well on your Quick Wins journey.

Paulie and Manny

Quick Wins

References

Alimo-Metcalfe, B. (1998) 360 degree feedback and leadership development. *International Journal of Selection & Assessment*, 6, 1, 35-44.

Austin, J. (2000). Performance analysis and performance diagnostics. In J. Austin & J. Carr (Eds.), *Handbook of applied behavior analysis* (pp. 304–327). Reno, NV: Context Press.

Bandura, A. (1977). Social learning theory. In B. B. Wolman & L. R. Pomroy (Eds.), *International encyclopedia of psychiatry, psychology, psychoanalysis, and neurology* (Vol. 10). New York: Van Nostrand Reinhold.

Bandura, A. (1986). The explanatory and predictive scope of self-efficacy theory. *Journal of Clinical and Social Psychology, 4,* 359–373.

Bandura, A. (1997). *Self-efficacy: The exercise of control.* New York, NY: Freeman.

Daniels, A. C. (2016). *Bringing out the best in people: How to apply the astonishing power of positive reinforcement.* New York, NY: McGraw-Hill Education; 3d edition.

Daniels, A. C., and Daniels, J. E. (2007). *Measure of a leader: The legendary leadership formula for producing exceptional performers and outstanding results.* New York, NY: McGraw-Hill Education.

Edwards, J. R. (1996). An examination of competing versions of the person-environment fit approach to stress. *Academy of Management Journal*, 39, 292-339.

Gavoni, P., Edmonds, W. A., & Kennedy, T. D., Gollery, T. (in press). Data on the data: A method for improving the fidelity of office discipline referral completion. *The Journal of Teacher Action Research.*

Geller, E. S. (2003). Should organizational behavior management expand its content? *Journal of Organizational Behavior Management, 22*(2), 13–30. doi:10.1300/J075v22n02_03

Goman, C. K. (2011). *The silent language of leaders.* San Francisco, CA: Jossey-Bass.

Gray, S. P., & Streshly, W. A. (2008). *From good schools to great schools: What their principals do well.* Thousand Oaks, CA: Corwin Press.

Grissom, J. A., & Harrington. J. R. (2010). Investing in administrator efficacy: An examination of professional development as a tool for enhancing principal effectiveness. *American Journal of Education* 116(4): 583-612

Hersey, P., Blanchard, K. H., & Johnson, D. E. (2001). *Management of organizational behavior: Leading human resources* (8th ed.). Upper Saddle River, NJ: Prentice-Hall.

Kramer, A., et al. (2014-06-17). "Experimental evidence of massive-scale emotional contagion through social networks." PNAS. 111 (24): 8788–8790. doi:10.1073/pnas.1320040111 PMID 24889601

Krapfl, J. E., & Kruja, B. (2015). Leadership and Culture. *Journal of Organizational Behavior Management, 35*:1–2, 28–43.

Laipple, J. (2012). *Rapid change: Immediate action for the impatient leader.* Atlanta, GA: Performance Management Publication (Aubrey Daniels, Inc.).

Latham, G. (1998). *Keys to Classroom Management.* North Logan, UT: P & T ink, publisher

Moore, B. (2009). Improving the Evaluation and Feedback Process for Principals. *Principal.* Retrieved from naesp.org

Parsons, M. B., Rollyson, J. H., & Reid, D. H. (2013). Teaching practitioners to conduct behavioral skills training: a pyramidal approach for training multiple human service staff. *Behavior Analysis in Practice, 6,* 4–16.

Rebore, R. W. (2012). *The essentials of human resources administration in education.* Boston, MA:

Pearson-Rogers, C.R. (1956). Client-centered therapy: A current view. In F. Fromm-Reichmann & J.L. Moreno (Eds.). *Progress in psychotherapy* (pp. 199-209). New York: Grune and Stratton.

Joyce, B., & Showers, B. (2002). *Student achievement through staff development* (3rd ed.). Alexandria, VA: Association for Supervision and Curriculum Development.

Supovitz, J., Foley, E., & Mishook, J. (2012). In search of leading indicators in education. *Education Policy Analysis Archives, 20,* 19. doi:http://dx.doi.org/10.14507/epaa.v20n19.2012

The Doing What Works Library. (2015, March 19). Retrieved July 25, 2016, from http://dwwlibrary.wested.org/library/4-quick-wins.

Vroom, V. H., & Jago, A. G. (2007). The role of the situation in leadership. *American Psychologist, 62*(1), 17-24.

Author Bios

Paul "Paulie" Gavoni, Ed.D.

Dr. Paul Gavoni has successfully supported multiple struggling schools in the turnaround process. An expert in human performance and organizational leadership, Paul enjoys supporting district and school leaders with developing behavior and performance management systems aimed at bringing out the best in educators and students. Paul is also a highly respected coach in combat sports. Paul began boxing in South Florida and went on to win a Florida Golden Gloves Heavyweight Title in 1998. Coach "Paulie Gloves," has trained many champions and UFC vets using techniques rooted in the behavioral sciences. Paul is a featured coach in the book *Beast: Blood, Struggle, and Dreams at the Heart of Mixed Martial Arts* by Doug Merlino. You can find other works by Paulie in online magazines such as *Scifighting* and *Last Word on Sports*.

Manuel "Manny" Rodriguez, M.S.

Manny has worked with many organizations across the globe. He is an accomplished Organizational Behavior Management practitioner, working with leaders across multiple industries and some of the largest organizations in the world. He has held leadership positions as an external consultant, and as a Global Environmental Health and Safety leader for a major chemical company. Today, Manny is Vice President for ABA Technologies, Inc., a leader in professional development, training and consulting in the field of behavior analysis. Manny has authored several articles disseminating the science of behavior applied at work, and is co-author of the book *OBM Applied! A Practical Guide to Implementing Organizational Behavior Management*. When Manny is not working, he is giving back to the larger professional field of behavior analysis, serving as a member and on the board of directors for the Organizational Behavior Management Network, teaching at various universities, and mentoring young professionals.